The Power of Concentration

Theron Q. Dumont

TUTIS Digital Publishing Pvt Ltd

ISBN 978-81-8456-161-6

The Power of Concentration

This impression 2007

Published by

TUTIS Digital Publishing Pvt Ltd.

26 Ramasamy Street

T. Nagar, Chennai 600 017

CONTENTS

Introductory

We all know that in order to accomplish a certain thing we must concentrate. It is of the utmost value to learn how to concentrate. To make a success of anything you must be able to concentrate your entire thought upon the idea you are working out.

Do not become discouraged, if you are unable to hold your thought on the subject very long at first. There are very few that can. It seems a peculiar fact that it is easier to concentrate on something that is not good for us, than on something that is beneficial. This tendency is overcome when we learn to concentrate consciously.

If you will just practice a few concentration exercises each day you will find you will soon develop this wonderful power.

Success is assured when you are able to concentrate for you are then able to utilize for your good all constructive thoughts and shut out all the destructive ones. It is of the greatest value to be able to think only that which will be beneficial.

Did you ever stop to think what an important part your thoughts, concentrated thoughts, play in your life? This book shows their far-reaching and all-abiding effects.

These lessons you will find very practical. The exercises I have thoroughly tested. They are arranged so that you will notice an improvement from the very start, and this will give you encouragement. They point out ways in which you can help yourself.

Man is a wonderful creature, but he must be trained and developed to be useful. A great work can be accomplished by every man if he can be awakened to do his very best. But the greatest man would not accomplish much if he lacked concentration and effort. Dwarfs can often do the work of giants when they are transformed by the almost magic power of great mental concentration. But giants will only do the work of dwarfs when they lack this power.

We accomplish more by concentration than by fitness; the man that is apparently best suited for a place does not always fill it best. It is the man that concentrates on its every possibility that makes an art of both his work and his life.

All your real advancement must come from your individual effort.

This course of lessons will stimulate and inspire you to achieve success; it will bring you into perfect harmony with the laws of success. It will give you a firmer hold on your duties and responsibilities.

The methods of thought concentration given in this work if put into practice will open up interior avenues that will connect you with the everlasting laws of Being and their exhaustless foundation of unchangeable truth.

As most people are very different it is impossible to give instructions that will be of the same value to all. The author has endeavored in these lessons to awaken that within the soul which perhaps the book does not express. So study these lessons as a means of awakening and training that which is within yourself. Let all your acts and thoughts have the intensity and power of concentration.

To really get the full benefit of these lessons you should read a page, then close the book and thoughtfully recall its ideas. If you will do this you will soon cultivate a concentrated mental habit, which will enable you to read with ordinary rapidity and remember all that you read.

LESSON I

Concentration Finds the Way

Everyone has two natures. One wants us to advance and the other wants to pull us back. The one that we cultivate and concentrate on decides what we are at the end. Both natures are trying to gain control. The will alone decides the issue. A man by one supreme effort of the will may change his whole career and almost accomplish miracles. You may be that man. You can be if you Will to be, for Will can find a way or make one.

I could easily fill a book, of cases where men plodding along in a matter-of-fact way, were all at once aroused and as if awakening from a slumber they developed the possibilities within them and from that time on were different persons. You alone can decide when the turning point will come. It is a matter of choice whether we allow our diviner self to control us or whether we will be controlled by the brute within us. No man has to do anything he does not want to do. He is therefore the director of his life if he wills to be. What we are to do, is the result of our training. We are like putty, and can be completely controlled by our will power.

Habit is a matter of acquirement. You hear people say: "He comes by this or that naturally, a chip off the old block," meaning that he is only doing what his parents did. This is quite often the case, but there is no reason for it, for a person can break a habit just the moment he masters the "I will." A man may have been a "good-for-nothing" all his life up to this very minute, but from this time on he begins to amount to something. Even old men have suddenly changed and accomplished wonders. "I lost my opportunity," says one. That may be true, but by sheer force of will, we can find a way to bring us another opportunity. There is no truth in the saying that opportunity knocks at our door but once in a lifetime. The fact is, opportunity never seeks us; we must seek it. What usually turns out to be one man's opportunity, was another man's loss. In this day one man's brain is matched against another's. It is often the quickness of brain action that determines the result. One man thinks "I will do it," but while he procrastinates the other goes ahead and does the work. They both have the same opportunity. The one will complain of his lost chance. But it should teach him a lesson, and it will, if he is seeking the path that leads to success.

Many persons read good books, but say they do not get much good out of them. They do not realize that all any book or any lesson course can do is to awaken them to their possibilities; to stimulate them to use their will power. You may teach a person from now until doom's day, but that person will only know what he learns himself. "You can lead him to the fountain, but you can't make him drink."

One of the most beneficial practices I know of is that of looking for the good in everyone and everything, for there is good in all things. We encourage a person by seeing his good qualities and we also help ourselves by looking for them. We gain their good wishes, a most valuable asset sometimes. We get back what we give out. The time comes when most all of us need encouragement; need buoying up. So form the habit of encouraging others, and you will find it a wonderful tonic for both those encouraged and yourself, for you will get back encouraging and uplifting thoughts.

Life furnishes us the opportunity to improve. But whether we do it or not depends upon how near we live up to what is expected of us. The first of each month, a person should sit down and examine the progress he has made. If he has not come up to "expectations" he should discover the reason, and by extra exertion measure up to what is demanded next time. Every time that we fall behind what we planned to do, we lose just so much for that time is gone forever. We may find a reason for doing it, but most excuses are poor substitutes for action. Most things are possible. Ours may be a hard task, but the harder the task, the greater the reward. It is the difficult things that really develop us, anything that requires only a small effort, utilizes very few of our faculties, and yields a scanty harvest of achievement. So do not shrink from a hard task, for to accomplish one of these will often bring us more good than a dozen lesser triumphs.

I know that every man that is willing to pay the price can be a success. The price is not in money, but in effort. The first essential quality for success is the desire to do—to be something. The next thing is to learn how to do it; the next to carry it into execution. The man that is the best able to accomplish anything is the one with a broad mind; the man that has acquired knowledge, that may, it is true, be foreign to this particular case, but is, nevertheless, of some value in all cases. So the man that wants to be successful must be liberal; he must acquire all the knowledge that he can; he must be well posted not only in one branch of his business but in every part of it. Such a man achieves success.

The secret of success is to try always to improve yourself no matter where you are or what your position. Learn all you can. Don't see how little you can do, but how much you can do. Such a man will always be in demand, for he establishes the reputation of being a hustler. There is always room for him because progressive firms never let a hustler leave their employment if they can help it.

The man that reaches the top is the gritty, plucky, hard worker and never the timid, uncertain, slow worker. An untried man is seldom put in a position of responsibility and power. The man selected is one that has done something, achieved results in some line, or taken the lead in his department. He is placed there because of his reputation of putting vigor and virility into his efforts, and because he has previously shown that he has pluck and determination.

The man that is chosen at the crucial time is not usually a genius; he does not possess any more talent than others, but he has learned that results can only be produced by untiring concentrated effort. That "miracles," in business do not just "happen." He knows that the only way they will happen is by sticking to a proposition and seeing it through. That is the only secret of why some succeed and others fail. The successful man gets used to seeing things accomplished and always feels sure of success. The man that is a failure gets used to seeing failure, expects it and attracts it to him.

It is my opinion that with the right kind of training every man could be a success. It is really a shame that so many men and women, rich in ability and talent, are allowed to go to waste, so to speak. Some day I hope to see a millionaire philanthropist start a school for the training of failures. I am sure he could not put his money to a better use. In a year's time the science of practical psychology could do wonders for him. He could have agencies on the lookout for men that had lost their grip on themselves; that had through indisposition weakened their will; that through some sorrow or misfortune had become discouraged. At first all they need is a little help to get them back on their feet, but usually they get a knock downwards instead. The result is that their latent powers never develop and both they and the world are the losers. I trust that in the near future, someone will heed the opportunity of using some of his millions in arousing men that have begun to falter. All they need to be shown is that there is within them an omnipotent source that is ready to aid them, providing they will make use of it. Their minds only have to be turned from despair to hope to make them regain their hold.

When a man loses his grip today, he must win his redemption by his own will. He will get little encouragement or advice of an inspiring nature. He must usually regain the right road alone. He must stop dissipating his energies and turn his attention to building a useful career. Today we must conquer our weakening tendencies alone. Don't expect anyone to help you. Just take one big brace, make firm resolutions, and resolve to conquer your weaknesses and vices. Really none can do this for you. They can encourage you; that is all.

I can think of nothing, but lack of health, that should interfere with one becoming successful. There is no other handicap that you should not be able to overcome. To overcome a handicap, all that it is necessary to do is to use more determination and grit and will.

The man with grit and will, may be poor today and wealthy in a few years; will power is a better asset than money; Will will carry you over chasms of failure, if you but give it the chance.

The men that have risen to the highest positions have usually had to gain their victories against big odds. Think of the hardships many of our inventors have gone through before they became a success. Usually they have been very much misunderstood by relatives and friends. Very often they did not have the bare necessities of life, yet, by sheer determination and resolute courage, they managed to exist somehow until they perfected their inventions, which afterwards greatly helped in bettering the condition of others.

Everyone really wants to do something, but there are few that will put forward the needed effort to make the necessary sacrifice to secure it. There is only one way to accomplish anything and that is to go ahead and do it. A man may accomplish almost anything today, if he just sets his heart on doing it and lets nothing interfere with his progress. Obstacles are quickly overcome by the man that sets out to accomplish his heart's desire. The "bigger" the man, the smaller the obstacle appears. The "smaller" the man the greater the obstacle appears. Always look at the advantage you gain by overcoming obstacles, and it will give you the needed courage for their conquest.

Do not expect that you will always have easy sailing. Parts of your journey are likely to be rough. Don't let the rough places put you out of commission. Keep on with the journey. Just the way you weather the storm shows what material you are made of. Never sit down and complain of the rough places, but think how nice the pleasant stretches were. View with delight the smooth plains that are in front of you.

Do not let a setback stop you. Think of it as a mere incident that has to be overcome before you can reach your goal.

LESSON II

The Self-Mastery: Self-Direction Power of Concentration

Man from a psychological standpoint of development is not what he should be. He does not possess the self-mastery, the self-directing power of concentration that is his by right.

He has not trained himself in a way to promote his self-mastery. Every balanced mind possesses the faculties whose chief duties are to engineer, direct and concentrate the operations of the mind, both in a mental and physical sense. Man must learn to control not only his mind but his bodily movements.

When the controlling faculties (autonomic) are in an untrained condition, the impulses, passions, emotions, thoughts, actions and habits of the person suffer from lack of regulation, and the procedure of mental concentration is not good, not because the mind is necessarily weak in the autonomic department of the faculties, but because the mind is not properly trained.

When the self-regulating faculties are not developed the impulses, appetites, emotions and passions have full swing to do as they please and the mind becomes impulsive, restless, emotional and irregular in its action. This is what makes mental concentration poor.

When the self-guiding faculties are weak in development, the person always lacks the power of mental concentration. Therefore you cannot learn to concentrate until you develop those very powers that qualify you to be able to concentrate. So if you cannot concentrate one of the following is the cause:

1. "Deficiency of the motor centers."
2. "An impulsive and emotional mind."
3. "An untrained mind."

The last fault can soon be removed by systematic practice. It is easiest to correct.

The impulsive and emotional state of mind can best be corrected by restraining anger, passion and excitement, hatred, strong impulses, intense emotions, fretfulness, etc. It is impossible to concentrate when you are in any of these excited states.

These can be naturally decreased by avoiding such food and drinks as have nerve weakening or stimulating influences, or a tendency to stir up the passions, the impulses and the emotions; it is a very good practice to watch and associate with those persons that are steady, calm, controlled and conservative.

Correcting the deficiency of the motor centers is harder because as the person's brain is undeveloped he lacks will power.

To cure this takes some time. Persons so afflicted may benefit by reading and studying my course, "The Master Mind."[*]

Many have the idea that when they get into a negative state they are concentrating, but this is not so. They may be meditating, though not concentrating. Those that are in a negative state a good deal of the time cannot, as a rule, concentrate very well; they develop instead abstraction of the mind, or absence of mind. Their power of concentration becomes weaker and they find it difficult to concentrate on anything. They very often injure the brain, if they keep up this state. To be able to concentrate you must possess strength of mind. The person that is feeble-minded cannot concentrate his mind, because of lack of will. The mind that cannot center itself on a special subject, or thought, is weak; also the mind that cannot draw itself from a subject or thought is weak. But the person that can center his mind on any problem, no matter what it is, and remove any unharmonious impressions has strength of mind. Concentration, first, last and all the time, means strength of mind.

Through concentration a person is able to collect and hold his mental and physical energies at work. A concentrated mind pays attention to thoughts, words, acts and plans. The person who allows his mind to roam at will will never accomplish a great deal in the world. He wastes his energies. If you work, think, talk and act aimlessly, and allow your brain to wander from your subject to foreign fields, you will not be able to concentrate. You concentrate at the moment when you say, "I want to, I can, I will."

Some Mistakes Some People Make. If you waste your time reading sensational stories or worthless newspaper items, you

[*]To be published by Advanced Thought Publishing Co., Chicago, Ill.

excite the impulsive and the emotional faculties, and this means you are weakening your power of concentration. You will not be a free engineer, able to pilot yourself to success.

Concentration of the mind can only be developed by watching yourself closely. All kinds of development commence with close attention. You should regulate your every thought and feeling. When you commence to watch yourself and your own acts and also the acts of other people, you use the faculties of autonomy, and, as you continue to do so, you improve your faculties, until in time you can engineer your every thought, wish and plan. To be able to focalize the mind on the object at hand in a conscious manner leads to concentration. Only the trained mind can focalize. To hold a thought before it until all the faculties shall have had time to consider that thought is concentration.

The person that cannot direct his thoughts, wishes, plans, resolutions and studies cannot possibly succeed to the fullest extent. The person that is impulsive one moment and calm the next has not the proper control over himself. He is not a master of his mind, nor of his thoughts, feelings and wishes. Such a person cannot be a success. When he becomes irritated, he irritates others and spoils all chances of any concerned doing their best. But the person that can direct his energies and hold them at work in a concentrated manner controls his every work and act, and thereby gains power to control others. He can make his every move serve a useful end and every thought a noble purpose.

In this day the man that gets excited and irritable should be looked upon as an undesirable person. The person of good breeding now speaks with slowness and deliberation. He is cultivating more and more of a reposeful attitude. He is consciously attentive and holds his mind to one thing at a time. He shuts out everything else. When you are talking to anyone give him your sole and undivided attention. Do not let your attention wander or be diverted. Give no heed to anything else, but make your will and intellect act in unison.

Start out in the morning and see how self-poised you can remain all day. At times take an inventory of your actions during the day and see if you have kept your determination. If not, see that you do tomorrow. The more self-poised you are the better will your concentration be. Never be in too much of a hurry; and, remember, the more you improve your concentration, the greater are your possibilities. Concentration means success, because you are better able to govern yourself and centralize your mind; you become more in earnest in what you do and this almost invariably improves your chances for success.

When you are talking to a person have your own plans in mind. Concentrate your strength upon the purpose you are talking about. Watch his every move, but keep your own plans before you. Unless you do, you will waste your energy and not accomplish as much as you should.

I want you to watch the next person you see that has the reputation of being a strong character, a man of force. Watch and see what a perfect control he has over his body. Then I want you to watch just an ordinary person. Notice how he moves his eyes, arms, fingers; notice the useless expenditure of energy. These movements all break down the vital cells and lessen the person's power in vital and nerve directions. It is just as important for you to conserve your nervous forces as it is the vital forces. As an example we see an engine going along the track very smoothly. Some one opens all the valves and the train stops. It is the same with you. If you want to use your full amount of steam, you must close your valves and direct your power of generating mental steam toward one end. Center your mind on one purpose, one plan, one transaction.

There is nothing that uses up nerve force so quickly as excitement. This is why an irritable person is never magnetic; he is never admired or loved; he does not develop those finer qualities that a real gentleman possesses. Anger, sarcasm and excitement weaken a person in this direction. The person that allows himself to get excited will become nervous in time, because he uses up his nerve forces and his vital energies. The person that cannot control himself and keep from becoming excited cannot concentrate.

When the mind can properly concentrate, all the energy of every microscopic cell is directed into one channel and then there is a powerful personal influence generated. Everyone possesses many millions of little trembling cells, and each one of these has a center where life and energy are stored up and generated. If this energy is not wasted but conserved and controlled, this person is influential, but when it is the opposite, he is not influential or successful.

Just as it is impossible for a steam engine to run with all its valves open, so is it impossible for you to waste your energy and run at your top speed. Each neuron in the gray layers of the brain is a psychic center of thought and action, each one is pulsating an intelligent force of some kind, and when this force, your thoughts and motions, are kept in cheek by a conservative, systematic and concentrated mind, the result will be magnetism, vitality and health. The muscles, bones, ligaments, feet, hands and nerves, etc., are agents for carrying out the mandates of the mind. The sole purpose of the volitional faculties is to move the physical mechanism as the energy travels along the wires of nerves and muscles. Just for that reason, if you throw a voluntary control over these messages, impulses, thoughts, emotions, physical movements and over these physical instruments you develop your faculties of self-mastery and to the extent you succeed here in proportion will you develop the power of concentration.

Any exercise or work that excites the mind, stimulates the senses, calls the emotions and appetites into action, confuses, terrifies or emotionalizes, weakens the power of concentration. This is why all kind of excitement is bad. This is the reason why persons who drink strong drinks, who allow themselves to get into fits of temper, who fight, who eat stimulating food, who sing and dance and thus develop their emotions, who are sudden, vehement and emotional, lack the power to concentrate. But those whose actions are slower and directed by their intelligence develop concentration. Sometimes dogmatic, wilful, excitable persons can concentrate, but it is spasmodic, erratic concentration instead of controlled and uniform concentration. Their energy works by spells; sometimes they have plenty, other times very little; it is easily excited; easily wasted. The best way to understand it is to compare it with the discharge of a gun. If the gun goes off when you want it to, it accomplishes the purpose, but if it goes off before you are ready for it, you will not only waste ammunition, but it is also likely to do some damage. That is just what most persons do. They allow their energy to explode, thus not only wasting it but endangering others. They waste their power, their magnetism and so injure their chance of success. Such persons are never well liked and never will be until they gain control over themselves.

It will be necessary for them to practice many different kinds of concentration exercises, and to keep them up for some time. They must completely overcome their sudden, erratic thoughts, and regulate their emotions and movements. They must from morning to night train the mind to be steady, and direct and keep the energies at work.

The lower area of the brain is the store house of the energy. Most all persons have all the dynamic energy they need if they would concentrate it. They have the machine, but they must also have the engineer, or they will not go very far. The engineer is the self-regulating, directing power. The person that does not develop his engineering qualities will not accomplish much in life. The good engineer controls his every act. All work assists in development. By what you do you either advance or degenerate. This is a good idea to keep always in mind. When you are uncertain whether you should do something or not, just think whether by doing it you will grow or deteriorate, and act accordingly.

I am a firm believer in "work when you work, and play when you play." When you give yourself up to pleasure you can develop concentration by thinking of nothing else but pleasure; when your mind dwells on love, think of nothing but this and you will find you can develop a more intense love than you ever had before. When you concentrate your mind on the "you" or real self, and its wonderful possibilities, you develop concentration and a higher opinion of yourself. By doing this systematically, you develop much power, because you cannot be systematic without concentrating on what you are doing. When you walk out into the country and inhale the fresh air, studying vegetation, trees, etc., you are concentrating. When you see that you are at your place of business at a certain time each morning you are developing steadiness of habit and becoming systematic. If you form the habit of being on time one morning, a little late the next, and still later the following one, you are not developing concentration, but whenever you fix your mind on a certain thought and hold your mind on it at successive intervals, you develop concentration.

If you hold your mind on some chosen object, you centralize your attention, just like the lens of the camera centralizes on a certain landscape. Therefore always hold your mind on what you are doing, no matter what it is. Keep a careful watch over yourself, for unless you do your improvement will be very slow.

Practice inhaling long, deep breaths, not simply for the improvement of health, although that is no small matter, but also for the purpose of developing more power, more love, more life. All work assists in development.

You may think it foolish to try to develop concentration by taking muscular exercises, but you must not forget that the mind is associated with muscle and nerve. When you steady your nerves and muscles, you steady your mind, but let your nerves get out of order and your mind will become erratic and you will not possess the power of direction, which, in other words, is concentration. Therefore you understand how important exercises that steady the nerves and muscles are in developing concentration.

Everyone is continually receiving impulses that must be directed and controlled if one is to lead a successful life. That is the reason why a person must control the movements of his eyes, feet, fingers, etc.; this is another reason why it is important to control his breathing. The slow, deep, prolonged exhalations are of wonderful value. They steady the circulation, the heart action, muscles and nerves of the mind. If the heart flutters, the circulation is not regular, and when the lung action is uneven, the mind becomes unsteady and not fit for concentration. This is why controlled breathing is very important as a foundation for physical health.

You must not only concentrate your mind, but also the action of the eyes, ears and fingers. Each of these contain miniature minds that are controlled by the master engineer. You will develop much quicker if you thoroughly realize this.

If you have ever associated with big men, or read their biographies, you will find that they usually let the others do the talking. It is much easier to talk than it is to listen. There is no better exercise for concentration than to pay close attention when some one is talking. Besides learning from what they have to say, you may develop both mental and physical concentration.

When you shake hands with some one just think of your hand as containing hundreds of individual minds, each having an intelligence of its own. When you put this feeling into your hand shake it shows personality. When you shake hands in a listless way, it denotes timidity, lack of force and power of personality. When the hand grip is very weak and stiff, the person has little love in his nature, no passion and no magnetism. When the hand shake is just the opposite, you will find that the nature is also. The loveless person is non-magnetic and he shows that he is by his non-magnetic hand shake. When two developed souls shake hands, their clasps are never light. There is a thrill that goes through both when the two currents meet. Love arouses the opposite currents of the positive and negative natures. When there is no love, life loses its charm. The hand quickly shows when love is being aroused. This is why you should study the art of hand shaking and develop your social affections. A person that loves his kind reflects love, but a person that hates reflects hate. The person with a bad nature, a hateful disposition, evil thoughts and feeling is erratic, freakish and fitful. When you allow yourself to become irritable, watch how you breathe and you will learn a valuable lesson. Watch how you breathe when you are happy. Watch your breathing when you harbor hate. Watch how you breathe when you feel in love with the whole world and noble emotions thrill you. When filled with good thoughts, you breathe a plentiful supply of oxygen into your lungs and love fills your soul. Love develops a person, physically, mentally and socially. Breathe deeply when you are happy and you will gain life and strength; you will steady your mind and you will develop your power of concentration and become magnetic and powerful.

If you want to get more out of life you must think more of love. Unless you have real affection for something, you have no sentiment, no sweetness, no magnetism. So arouse your love affections by your will and enter into a fuller life.

The hand of love always magnetizes, but it must be steady and controlled. Love can be concentrated in your hand shake, and this is one of the best ways to influence another.

The next time you feel yourself becoming irritable, use your will and be patient. This is a very good exercise in self-control. It will help you to keep patient if you will breathe slowly and deeply. If you find you are commencing to speak fast, just control yourself and speak slowly and clearly. Keep from either raising or lowering your voice and concentrate on the fact that you are determined to keep your poise, and you will improve your power of concentration.

When you meet people of some consequence, assume a reposeful attitude before them. Do this at all times. Watch both them and yourself. Static exercises develop the motor faculties and increase the power of concentration. If you feel yourself getting irritable, nervous or weak, stand squarely on your feet with your chest up and inhale deeply and you will see that your irritability will disappear and a silent calm will pass over you.

If you are in the habit of associating with nervous, irritable people, quit it until you grow strong in the power of concentration, because irritable, angry, fretful, dogmatic and disagreeable people will weaken what powers of resistance you have.

Any exercises that give you better control of the ears, fingers, eyes, feet, help you to steady your mind; when your eye is steady, your mind is steady. One of the best ways to study a person is to watch his physical movements, for, when we study his actions, we are studying his mind. Because actions are the expressions of the mind. As the mind is, so is the action. If it is uneasy, restless, erratic, unsteady, its actions are the same. When it is composed, the mind is composed. Concentration means control of the mind and body. You cannot secure control over one without the other.

Many people who seem to lack ambition have sluggish minds. They are steady, patient and seemingly have good control, but this does not say they are able to concentrate. These people are indolent, inactive, slow and listless, because they lack energy; they do not lose control because they have little force to control. They have no temper and it therefore cannot disturb them. Their actions are steady because they possess little energy. The natural person is internally strong, energetic and forceful, but his energy, force and strength, thoughts and physical movements are well under his control.

If a person does not have energy, both mental and physical, he must develop it. If he has energy which he cannot direct and hold to a point he must learn to do so. A man may be very capable, but, unless he Wills to control his abilities, they will not do him any good.

We hear so much talk about the benefit of physical culture, but the real benefit of this is really lost sight of. There is nothing that holds the faculties at work in a sustained and continuous manner as static exercises do. For, as stated before, when you learn to control the body, you are gaining control over the mind.

LESSON III

How to Gain What You Want Through Concentration

The ignorant person may say, "How can you get anything by merely wanting it? I say that through concentration you can get anything you want. Every desire can be gratified. But whether it is, will depend upon you concentrating to have that desire fulfilled. Merely wishing for something will not bring it. Wishing you had something shows a weakness and not a belief that you will really get it. So never merely wish, as we are not living in a "fairy age." You use up just as much brain force in "vain imaginings" as you do when you think of something worth while.

Be careful of your desires, make a mental picture of what you want and set your will to this until it materializes. Never allow yourself to drift without helm or rudder. Know what you want to do, and strive with all your might to do it, and you will succeed.

Feel that you can accomplish anything you undertake. Many undertake to do things, but feel when they start they are going to fail and usually they do. I will give an illustration. A man goes to a store for an article. The clerk says, "I am sorry, we have not it." But the man that is determined to get that thing inquires if he doesn't know where he can get it. Again receiving an unsatisfactory answer the determined buyer consults the manager and finally he finds where the article can be bought.

That is the whole secret of concentrating on getting what you want. And, remember, your soul is a center of all-power, and you can accomplish what you will to. "I'll find a way or make one!" is the spirit that wins. I know a man that is now head of a large bank. He started there as a messenger boy. His father had a button made for him with a "P" on it and put it on his coat. He said, "Son, that 'P' is a reminder that some day you are to be the president of your bank. I want you to keep this thought in your mind. Every day do something that will put you nearer your goal." Each night after supper he would say, "Son, what did you do today?" In this way the thought was always kept in mind. He concentrated on becoming president of that bank, and he did. His father told him never to tell anyone what that "P" stood for. A good deal of fun was made of it by his associates. And they tried to find out what it stood for, but they never did until he was made president and then he told the secret.

Don't waste your mental powers in wishes. Don't dissipate your energies by trying to satisfy every whim. Concentrate on doing something really worth while. The man that sticks to something is not the man that fails.

"Power to him who power exerts."—Emerson.

Success to-day depends largely on concentrating on the Interior law of force, for when you do this you awaken those thought powers or forces, which, when used in business, insures permanent results.

Until you are able to do this you have not reached your limit in the use of your forces. This great universe is interwoven with myriads of forces. You make your own place, and whether it is important depends upon you. Through the Indestructible and Unconquerable Law you can in time accomplish all right things and therefore do not be afraid to undertake whatever you really desire to accomplish and are willing to pay for in effort. Anything that is right is possible. That which is necessary will inevitably take place. If something is right it is your duty to do it, though the whole world thinks it to be wrong. "God and one are always a majority," or in plain words, that omnipotent interior law which is God, and the organism that represents you is able to conquer the whole world if your cause is absolutely just. Don't say I wish I was a great man. You can do anything that is proper and you want to do. Just say: You can. You will. You must. Just realize this and the rest is easy. You have the latent faculties and forces to subdue anything that tries to interfere with your plans.

"Let-the-troubles-and-responsibilities-of-life-come-thick-and-fas t. I-am-ready-for-them. My-soul-is-unconquerable. I-represent-the-Infinite-law-of-force,-or-of-all-power. This-God-within-is-my-all-sufficient-strength-and-ever-present-he lp-in-time-of-trouble. The-more-difficulties-the-greater-its-triumphs-through-me. The-harder-my-trials,-the-faster-I-go-in-the-development-of-my-in herent-strength. Let-all-else-fail-me. This-interior-reliance-is-all-sufficient. The-right-must-prevail. I-demand-wisdom-and-power-to-know-and-follow-the-right. My-higher-self-is-all-wise. I-now-draw-nearer-to-it.

LESSON IV

Concentration, the Silent Force that Produces Results in All Business

I want you first to realize how powerful thought is. A thought of fear has turned a person's hair gray in a night. A prisoner condemned to die was told that if he would consent to an experiment and lived through it he would be freed. He consented. They wanted to see how much blood a person could lose and still live. They arranged that blood would apparently drop from a cut made in his leg. The cut made was very slight, from which practically no blood escaped. The room was darkened, and the prisoner thought the dropping he heard was really coming from his leg. The next morning he was dead through mental fear.

The two above illustrations will give you a little idea of the power of thought. To thoroughly realize the power of thought is worth a great deal to you.

Through concentrated thought power you can make yourself whatever you please. By thought you can greatly increase your efficiency and strength. You are surrounded by all kinds of thoughts, some good, others bad, and you are sure to absorb some of the latter if you do not build up a positive mental attitude.

If you will study the needless moods of anxiety, worry, despondency, discouragement and others that are the result of uncontrolled thoughts, you will realize how important the control of your thoughts are. Your thoughts make you what you are.

When I walk along the street and study the different people's faces I can tell how they spent their lives. It all shows in their faces, just like a mirror reflects their physical countenances. In looking in those faces I cannot help thinking how most of the people you see have wasted their lives.

The understanding of the power of thought will awaken possibilities within you that you never dreamed of. Never forget that your thoughts are making your environment, your friends, and as your thoughts change these will also. Is this not a practical lesson to learn? Good thoughts are constructive. Evil thoughts are destructive. The desire to do right carries with it a great power. I want you to thoroughly realize the importance of your thoughts, and how to make them valuable, to understand that your thoughts come to you over invisible wires and influence you.

If your thoughts are of a high nature, you become connected with people of the same mental caliber and you are able to help yourself. If your thoughts are tricky, you will bring tricky people to deal with you, who will try to cheat you.

If your thoughts are right kind, you will inspire confidence in those with whom you are dealing.

As you gain the good will of others your confidence and strength will increase. You will soon learn the wonderful value of your thoughts and how serene you can become even when circumstances are the most trying.

Such thoughts of Right and Good Will bring you into harmony with people that amount to something in the world and that are able to give you help if you should need it, as nearly everyone does at times.

You can now see why it is so important to concentrate your thoughts in the proper channels. It is very necessary that people should have confidence in you. When two people meet they have not the time to look each other up. They accept each other according to instinct which can usually be relied on.

You meet a person and his attitude creates a suspicion in you. The chances are you cannot tell why, but something tells you, "Have no dealings with him, for if you do, you will be sorry." Thoughts produce actions. Therefore be careful of your thoughts. Your life will be molded by the thoughts you have. A spiritual power is always available to your thought, and when you are worthy you can attract all the good things without a great effort on your part.

The sun's rays shine down on our gardens, but we can plant trees that will interfere with the sun light. There are invisible forces ready to help you if you do not think and act to intercept these. These forces work silently. "You reap what you sow."

You have concentrated within powers that if developed will bring you happiness greater than you can even imagine. Most people go rushing through life, literally driving away the very things they seek. By concentration you can revolutionize your life, accomplish infinitely more and without a great effort.

Look within yourself and you will find the greatest machine ever made.

How to Speak Wisely. In order to speak wisely you must secure at least a partial concentration of the faculties and forces upon the subject at hand. Speech interferes with the focusing powers of the mind, as it withdraws the attention to the external and therefore is hardly to be compared with that deep silence of the subconscious mind, where deep thoughts, and the silent forces of high potency are evolved. It is necessary to be silent before you can speak wisely. The person that is really alert and well poised and able to speak wisely under trying circumstances, is the person that has practiced in the silence. Most people do not know what the silence is and think it is easy to go into the silence, but this is not so. In the real silence we become attached to that interior law and the forces become silent, because they are in a state of high potency, or beyond the vibratory sounds to which our external ears are attuned. He who desires to become above the ordinary should open up for himself the interior channels which lead to the absolute law of the omnipotent. You can only do this by persistently and intelligently practicing thought 0 thought:

In-silence-I-will-allow-my-higher-self-to-have-complete-control.
I-will-be-true-to-my-higher-self.
I-will-live-true-to-my-conception-of-what-is-right.
I-realize-that-it-is-to-my-self-interest-to-live-up-to-my-best.
I-demand-wisdom-so that-I-may-act-wisely-for-myself-and-others.

In the next chapter I will tell you of the mysterious law, which links all humanity together, by the powers of co-operative thought, and chooses for us companionship and friends.

LESSON V

How Concentrated Thought Links All Humanity Together

It is within your power to gratify your every wish. Success is the result of the way you think. I will show you how to think to be successful.

The power to rule and attract success is within yourself. The barriers that shut these off from you are subject to your control. You have unlimited power to think and this is the link that connects you with your omniscient source.

Success is the result of certain moods of mind or ways of thinking. These moods can be controlled by you and produced at will.

You have been evolved to what you are from a lowly atom because you possessed the power to think. This power will never leave you, but will keep urging you on until you reach perfection. As you evolve, you create new desires and these can be gratified. The power to rule lies within you. The barriers that keep you from ruling are also within you. These are the barriers of ignorance.

Concentrated thought will accomplish seemingly impossible results and make you realize your fondest ambitions. At the same time that you break down barriers of limitation new ambitions will be awakened. You begin to experience conscious thought constructions.

If you will just realize that through deep concentration you become linked with thoughts of omnipotence, you will kill out entirely your belief in your limitations and at the same time will drive away all fear and other negative and destructive thought forces which constantly work against you. In the place of these you will build up a strong assurance that your every venture will be successful. When you learn thus how to concentrate and reinforce your thought, you control your mental creations; they in turn help to mould your physical environment, and you become the master of circumstances and the ruler of your kingdom.It is just as easy to surround your life with what you want as it is with what you don't want. It is a question to be decided by your will. There are no walls to prevent you from getting what you want, providing you want what is right. If you choose something that is not right, you are in opposition to the omnipotent plans of the universe and deserve to fail. But, if you will base your desires on justice and good will, you avail yourself of the helpful powers of universal currents, and instead of having a handicap to work against, can depend upon ultimate success, though the outward appearances may not at first be bright.

Never stop to think of temporary appearances, but maintain an unfaltering belief in your ultimate success. Make your plans carefully, and see that they are not contrary to the tides of universal justice. The main thing for you to remember is to keep at bay the destructive and opposing forces of fear and anger and their satellites.

There is no power so great as the belief which comes from the knowledge that your thought is in harmony with the divine laws of thought and the sincere conviction that your cause is right. You may be able seemingly to accomplish results for a time even if your cause is unjust, but the results will be temporary, and, in time, you will have to tear down your thought edifice and build on the true foundation of Right.

Plans that are not built on truth produce discordant vibrations and are therefore self-destructive. Never try to build until you can build right. It is a waste of time to do anything else. You may temporarily put aside your desire to do right, but its true vibrations will interfere with your unjust plans until you are forced back into righteous paths of power.

All just causes succeed in time, though temporarily they may fail. So if you should face the time when everything seems against you, quiet your fears, drive away all destructive thoughts and uphold the dignity of your moral and spiritual life.

"Where There Is A Will There Is A Way." The reason this is so is that the Will can make a way if given the chance to secure the assistance of aiding forces. The more it is developed the higher the way to which it will lead.

When everything looks gloomy and discouraging, then is the time to show what you are made of by rejoicing that you can control your moods by making them as calm, serene and bright as if prosperity were yours.

"Be faithful in sowing the thought seeds of success, in perfect trust that the sun will not cease to shine and bring a generous harvest in one season."

It is not always necessary to think of the success of a venture when you are actually engaged in it. For when the body is inactive the mind is most free to catch new ideas that will further the opportunity you are seeking. When you are actually engaged in doing something, you are thinking in the channels you have previously constructed and the work does not have to be done over again.

When you are in a negative mood the intuitions are more active, for you are not then controlling your thoughts by the will. Everything we do. should have the approval of the intuition.

When you are in a negative mood you attract thoughts of similar nature through the law of affinity. That is why it is so important to form thoughts of a success nature to attract similar ones. If you have never made a study of this subject, you may think this is all foolishness, but it is a fact that there are thought currents that unerringly bring thoughts of a similar nature. Many persons who think of failure actually attract failure by their worries, their anxieties, their overactivity. These thoughts are bound to bring failure. When you once learn the laws of thought and think of nothing but Good, Truth, Success, you will make more progress with less effort than you ever made before.

There are forces that can aid the mind that are hardly dreamed of by the average person. When you learn to believe more in the value of thought and its laws you will be led aright and your business gains will multiply.

The following method may assist you in gaining better thought control. If you are unable to control your fears, just say to your faulty determination, "Do not falter or be afraid, for I am not really alone. I am surrounded by invisible forces that will assist me to remove the unfavorable appearances." Soon you will have more courage. The only difference between the fearless man and the fearful one is in his will, his hope. So if you lack success, believe in it, hope for it, claim it. You can use the same method to brace up your thoughts of desire, aspiration, imagination, expectation, ambition, understanding, trust and assurance.

If you get anxious, angry, discouraged, undecided or worried, it is because you are not receiving the co-operation of the higher powers of your mind. By your Will you can so organize the powers of the mind that your moods change only as you want them to instead of as circumstances affect you.

I was recently asked if I advised concentrating on what you eat, or what you see while walking. My reply was that no matter what you may be doing, when in practice think of nothing else but that act at the time. The idea is to be able to control your unimportant acts, otherwise you set up a habit that it will be hard to overcome, because your faculties have not been in the habit of concentrating. Your faculties cannot be disorganized one minute and organized the next. If you allow the mind to wander while you are doing small things, it will be likely to get into mischief and make it hard to concentrate on the important act when it comes.

The man that is able to concentrate is the happy, busy man. Time does not drag with him. He always has plenty to do. He does not have time to think over past mistakes, which would make him unhappy.

If despite our discouragement and failures, we claim our great heritage, "life and truth and force, like an electric current," will permeate our lives until we enter into our "birthright in eternity."

The will does not act with clearness, decision and promptness unless it is trained to do so. There are comparatively few that really know what they are doing every minute of the day. This is because they do not observe with sufficient orderliness and accuracy to know what they are doing. It is not difficult to know what you us doing all the time, if you will just practice concentration and with a reposeful deliberation, and train yourself to think clearly, promptly, and decisive. If you allow yourself to worry or hurry in what you are doing, this will not be clearly photographed upon the sensitized plate of the subjective mind, and you therefore will not be really conscious of your actions. So practice accuracy and concentration of thought, and also absolute truthfulness and you will soon be able to concentrate.

LESSON VI

The Training of the Will to Do

The Will To Do is the greatest power in the world that is concerned with human accomplishment and no one can in advance determine its limits.

The things that we do now would have been a few ages ago impossibilities. Today the safe maxim is: "All things are possible."

The Will To Do is a force that is strictly practical, yet it is difficult to explain just what it is. It can be compared to electricity because we know it only through its cause and effects. It is a power we can direct and to just the extent we direct it do we determine our future. Every time you accomplish any definite act, consciously or unconsciously, you use the principle of the Will. You can Will to do anything whether it is right or wrong, and therefore the way you use your will makes a big difference in your life.

Every person possesses some "Will To Do." It is the inner energy which controls all conscious acts. What you will to do directs your life forces. All habits, good or bad, are the result of what you will to do. You improve or lower your condition in life by what you will to do. Your will has a connection with all avenues of knowledge, all activities, all accomplishment.

You probably know of cases where people have shown wonderful strength under some excitement, similar to the following: The house of a farmer's wife caught on fire. No one was around to help her move anything. She was a frail woman, and ordinarily was considered weak. On this occasion she removed things from the house that it later took three men to handle. It was the "Will To Do" that she used to accomplish her task.

Genius Is But A Will To Do Little Things With Infinite Pains. Little Things Well Done Open The Door Of Opportunity For Bigger Things.

The Will accomplishes its greater results through activities that grow out of great concentration in acquiring the power of voluntary attention to such an extent that we can direct it where we will and hold it steadily to its task until our aim is accomplished. When you learn so to use it, your Will Power becomes a mighty force. Almost everything can be accomplished through its proper use. It is greater than physical force because it can be used to control not only physical but mental and moral forces.

There are very few that possess perfectly developed and balanced Will Power, but those who do easily crush out their weak qualities. Study yourself carefully. Find out your greatest weakness and then use your will power to overcome it. In this way eradicate your faults, one by one, until you have built up a strong character and personality.

Rules for Improvement. A desire arises. Now think whether this would be good for you. If it is not, use your Will Power to kill out the desire, but, on the other hand, if it is a righteous desire, summon all your Will Power to your aid, crush all obstacles that confront you and secure possession of the coveted Good.

Slowness in Making Decisions. This is a weakness of Will Power. You know you should do something, but you delay doing it through lack of decision. It is easier not to do a certain thing than to do it, but conscience says to do it. The vast majority of persons are failures because of the lack of deciding to do a thing when it should be done. Those that are successful have been quick to grasp opportunities by making a quick decision. This power of will can be used to bring culture, wealth and health.

Some Special Pointers. For the next week try to make quicker decisions in your little daily affairs. Set the hour you wish to get up and arise exactly at the fixed time. Anything that you should accomplish, do on or ahead of time. You want, of course, to give due deliberation to weighty matters, but by making quick decisions on little things you will acquire the ability to make quick decisions in bigger things. Never procrastinate. Decide quickly one way or the other even at the risk of deciding wrong. Practice this for a week or two and notice your improvement.

The Lack of Initiative. This, too, keeps many men from succeeding. They have fallen into the way of imitating others in all that they do. Very often we hear the expression, "He seems clever enough, but he lacks initiative." Life for them is one continuous grind. Day after day they go through the same monotonous round of duties, while those that are "getting along" are using their initiative to get greater fullness of life. There is nothing so responsible for poverty as this lack of initiative, this power to think and do for ourselves.

You Are as Good as Anyone. You have will power, and if you use it, you will get your share of the luxuries of life. So use it to claim your own. Don't depend on anyone else to help you. We have to fight our own battles. All the world loves a fighter, while the coward is despised by all.

Every person's problems are different, so I can only say "analyze your opportunities and conditions and study your natural abilities." Form plans for improvement and then put them into operation. Now, as I said before, don't just say, "I am going to do so and so," but carry your plan into execution. Don't make an indefinite plan, but a definite one, and then don't give up until your object has been accomplished. Put these suggestions into practice with true earnestness, and you will soon note astonishing results, and your whole life will be completely changed. An excellent motto for one of pure motives is: Through my will power I dare do what I want to. You will find this affirmation has a very strengthening effect.

The Spirit of Perseverance. The spirit of "sticktoitiveness" is the one that wins. Many go just so far and then give up, whereas, if they had persevered a little longer, they would have won out. Many have much initiative, but instead of concentrating it into one channel, they diffuse it through several, thereby dissipating it to such an extent that its effect is lost.

Develop more determination, which is only the Will To Do, and when you start out to do something stick to it until you get results. Of course, before starting anything you must look ahead and see what the "finish leads to." You must select a road that will lead to "somewhere," rather than "nowhere." The journey must be productive of some kind of substantial results. The trouble with so many young men is that they launch enterprises without any end in sight. It is not so much the start as the finish of a journey that counts. Each little move should bring you nearer the goal which you planned to reach before the enterprise began.

Lack of Perseverance is nothing but the lack of the Will To Do. It takes the same energy to say, "I will continue," as to say, "I give up." Just the moment you say the latter you shut off your dynamo, and your determination is gone. Every time you allow your determination to be broken you weaken it. Don't forget this. Just the instant you notice your determination beginning to weaken, concentrate on it and by sheer Will Power make it continue on the "job."

Never try to make a decision when you are not in a calm state of mind. If in a "quick temper," you are likely to say things you afterwards regret. In anger, you follow impulse rather than reason. No one can expect to achieve success if he makes decisions when not in full control of his mental forces.

Therefore make it a fixed rule to make decisions only when at your best. If you have a "quick temper," you can quickly gain control over it by simple rule of counting backwards. To count backwards requires concentration, and you thus quickly regain a calm state. In this way you can break the "temper habit."

It will do you a lot of good to think over what you said and thought the last time you were angry. Persevere until you see yourself as others see you. It would do no harm to write the scene out in story form and then sit in judgment of the character that played your part.

Special Instructions to Develop the Will To Do. This is a form of mental energy, but requires the proper mental attitude to make it manifest. We hear of people having wonderful will power, which really is wrong. It should be said that they use their will power while with many it is a latent force. I want you to realize that no one has a monopoly on will power. There is plenty for all. What we speak of as will power is but the gathering together of mental energy, the concentration power at one point. So never think of that person as having a stronger will than yours. Each person will be supplied with just that amount of will power that he demands. You don't have to develop will power if you constantly make use of all you have, and remember the way in which you use it determines your fate, for your life is moulded to great extent by the use you make of your will. Unless you make proper use of it you have neither independence nor firmness. You are unable to control yourself and become a mere machine for others to use. It is more important to learn to use your will than to develop your intellect. The man that has not learned how to use his will rarely decides things for himself, but allows his resolutions to be changed by others. He fluctuates from one opinion to another, and of course does not accomplish anything out of the ordinary, while his brother with the trained will takes his place among the world's leaders.

LESSON VII

The Concentrated Mental Demand

The Mental Demand is the potent force in achievement. The attitude of the mind affects the expression of the face, determines action, changes our physical condition and regulates our lives.

I will not here attempt to explain the silent force that achieves results. You want to develop your mental powers so you can effect the thing sought, and that is what I want to teach you. There is wonderful power and possibility in the concentrated Mental Demand. This, like all other forces, is controlled by laws. It can, like all other forces, be wonderfully increased by consecutive, systematized effort.

The mental demand must be directed by every power of the mind and every possible element should be used to make the demand materialize. You can so intently desire a thing that you can exclude all distracting thoughts. When you practice this singleness of concentration until you attain the end sought, you have developed a Will capable of accomplishing whatever you wish.

As long as you can only do the ordinary things you will be counted in the mass of mediocrity. But just as quick as you surpass others by even comparatively small measure, you are classed as one of life's successes. So, if you wish to emerge into prominence, you must accomplish something more than the ordinary man or woman. It is easy to do this if you will but concentrate on what you desire, and put forth your best effort. It is not the runner with the longest legs or the strongest muscles that wins the race, but the one that can put forth the greatest desire force. You can best understand this by thinking of an engine. The engine starts up slowly, the engineer gradually extending the throttle to the top notch. It is then keyed up to its maximum speed. The same is true of two runners. They start off together and gradually they increase their desire to go faster. The one that has the greatest intensity of desire will win. He may outdistance the other by only a fraction of an inch, yet he gets the laurels.

The men that are looked upon as the world's successes have not always been men of great physical power, nor at the start did they seem very well adapted to the conditions which encompassed them. In the beginning they were not considered men of superior genius, but they won their success by their resolution to achieve results in their undertakings by permitting no set-back to dishearten them; no difficulties to daunt them. Nothing could turn them or influence them against their determination. They never lost sight of their goal. In all of us there is this silent force of wonderful power. If developed, it can overcome conditions that would seem insurmountable. It is constantly urging us on to greater achievement. The more we become acquainted with it the better strategists we become, the more courage we develop and the greater the desire within us for self-expression in activity along many lines.

No one will ever be a failure if he becomes conscious of this silent force within that controls his destiny. But without the consciousness of this inner force, you will not have a clear vision, and external conditions will not yield to the power of your mind. It is the mental resolve that makes achievement possible. Once this has been formed it should never be allowed to cease to press its claim until its object is attained. To make plans work out it will, at times, be necessary to use every power of your mind. Patience, perseverance and all the indomitable forces within one will have to be mustered and used with the greatest effectiveness.

Perseverance is the first element of success. In order to persevere you must be ceaseless in your application. It requires you to concentrate your thoughts upon your undertaking and bring every energy to bear upon keeping them focused upon it until you have accomplished your aim. To quit short of this is to weaken all future efforts.

The Mental Demand seems an unreal power because it is intangible; but it is the mightiest power in the world. It is a power that is free for you to use. No one can use it for you. The Mental Demand is not a visionary one. It is a potent force, which you can use freely without cost. When you are in doubt it will counsel you. It will guide you when you are uncertain. When you are in fear it will give you courage. It is the motive power which supplies the energies necessary to the achievement of the purpose. You have a large store house of possibilities. The Mental Demand makes possibilities realities. It supplies everything necessary for the accomplishment, It selects the tools and instructs how to use them. It makes you understand the situation. Every time you make a Mental Demand you strengthen the brain centers by drawing to you external forces.

Few realize the power of a Mental Demand. It is possible to make your demand so strong that you can impart what you have to say to another without speaking to him. Have you ever, after planning to discuss a certain matter with a friend, had the experience of having him broach the subject before you had a chance to speak of it? Have you ever, in a letter, made a suggestion to a friend that he carried out before your letter reached him? Have you ever wanted to speak to a person who, just then walked in or telephoned. I have had many such responses to thought and you and your friends have doubtless experienced them, too.

These two things are neither coincidences nor accidents, but are the results of mental demand launched by strong concentration.

The person that never wants anything gets little. To demand resolutely is the first step toward getting what you want.

The power of the Mental Demand seems absolute, the supply illimitable. The mental demand projects itself and causes to materialize the conditions and opportunities needed to accomplish the purpose. Do not think I over estimate the value of the Mental Demand. It brings the fuller life if used for only righteous purposes. Once the Mental Demand is made, however, never let it falter. If you do the current that connects you with your desire is broken. Take all the necessary time to build a firm foundation, so that there need not be even an element of doubt to creep in. Just the moment you entertain "doubt" you lose some of the demand force, and force once lost is hard to regain. So whenever you make a mental demand hold steadfastly to it until your need is supplied.

I want to repeat again that Power of Mental Demand is not a visionary one. It is concentrated power only, and can be used by you. It is not supernatural power, but requires a development of the brain centers. The outcome is sure when it is given with a strong resolute determination.

No person will advance to any great extent, until he recognizes this force within him. If you have not become aware of it, you have not made very much of a success of your life. It is this "something" that distinguishes that "man" from other men. It is this subtle power that develops strong personality.

If you want a great deal you must demand a great deal. Once you make your demand, anticipate its fulfillment. It depends upon us. We are rewarded according to our efforts. The Power of Mental Demand can bring us what we want. We become what we determine to be. We control our own destiny.

Get the right mental attitude, then in accordance with your ability you can gain success.

And every man of AVERAGE ability, the ordinary man that you see about you, can be really successful, independent, free of worry, HIS OWN MASTER, if he can manage to do just two things.

First, remain forever dissatisfied with what he IS doing and with what he HAS accomplished.

Second, develop in his mind a belief that the word impossible was not intended or him. Build up in his mind the confidence that enables the mind to use its power.

Many, especially the older men, will ask:

"How can I build up that self-confidence in my brain? How can I, after months and years of discouragement, of dull plodding, suddenly conceive and carry out a plan for doing something that will mike life worth while and change the monotonous routine?

"How can a man get out of a rut after he has been in it for years and has settled down to the slow jog-trot that leads to the grave?"

The answer is the thing can be done, and millions have done it.

One of the names most honored among the great men of France is that of Littre, who wrote and compiled the great French dictionary—a monument of learning. He is the man whose place among the forty immortals of France was taken by the great Pasteur, when the latter was elected to the Academy.

Littre BEGAN the work that makes him famous when he was more than sixty years old.

LESSON VIII

Concentration Gives Mental Poise

You will find that the man that concentrates is well poised, whereas the man that allows his mind to wander is easily upset. When in this state wisdom does not pass from the subconscious storehouse into the consciousness. There must be mental quiet before the two consciousnesses can work in harmony. When you are able to concentrate you have peace of mind.

If you are in the habit of losing your poise, form the habit of reading literature that has a quieting power. Just the second you feel your poise slipping, say, "Peace," and then hold this thought in mind and you will never lose your self-control.

There cannot be perfect concentration until there is peace of mind. So keep thinking peace, acting peace, until you are at peace with all the world. For when once you have reached this state there will be no trouble to concentrate on anything you wish.

When you have peace of mind you are not timid or anxious, or fearful, or rigid and you will not allow any disturbing thought to influence you. You cast aside all fears, and think of yourself as a spark of the Divine Being, as a manifestation of the "One Universal Principle" that fills all space and time. Think of yourself thus as a child of the infinite, possessing infinite possibilities.

Write on a piece of paper, "I have the power to do and to be whatever I wish to do and be." Keep this mentally before you, and you will find the thought will be of great help to you.

The Mistake of Concentrating on Your Business While Away. In order to be successful today, you must concentrate, but don't become a slave to concentration, and carry your business cares home. Just as sure as you do you will be burning the life forces at both ends and the fire will go out much sooner than was intended.

Many men become so absorbed in their business that when they go to church they do not hear the preacher because their minds are on their business. If they go to the theater they do not enjoy it because their business is on their minds. When they go to bed they think about business instead of sleep and wonder why they don't sleep. This is the wrong kind of concentration and is dangerous. It is involuntary. When you are unable to get anything out of your mind it becomes unwholesome as any thought held continuously causes weariness of the flesh. It is a big mistake to let a thought rule you, instead of ruling it. He who does not rule himself is not a success. If you cannot control your concentration, your health will suffer.

So never become so absorbed with anything that you cannot lay it aside and take up another. This is self-control.

Concentration Is Paying Attention to a Chosen Thought. Everything that passes before the eye makes an impression on the subconscious mind, but unless you pay attention to some certain thing you will not remember what you saw. For instance if you walked down a busy street without seeing anything that attracted your particular attention, you could not recall anything you saw. So you see only what attracts your attention. If you work you only see and remember what you think about. When you concentrate on something it absorbs your whole thought.

Self-Study Valuable. Everyone has some habits that can be overcome by concentration. We will say for instance, you are in the habit of complaining, or finding fault with yourself or others; or, imagining that you do not possess the ability of others; or feeling that you are not as good as someone else; or that you cannot rely on yourself; or harboring any similar thoughts or thoughts of weakness. These should be cast aside and instead thoughts of strength should be put in their place. Just remember every time you think of yourself as being weak, in some way you are making yourself so by thinking you are. Our mental conditions make us what we are. Just watch yourself and see how much time you waste in worrying, fretting and complaining. The more of it you do the worse off you are.

Just the minute you are aware of thinking a negative thought immediately change to a positive one. If you start to think of failure, change to thinking of success. You have the germ of success within you. Care for it the same as the setting hen broods over the eggs and you can make it a reality.

You can make those that you come in contact with feel as you do, because you radiate vibrations of the way you feel and your vibrations are felt by others. When you concentrate on a certain thing you turn all the rays of your vibrations on this. Thought is the directing power of all Life's vibrations. If a person should enter a room with a lot of people and feel as if he were a person of no consequence no one would know he was there unless they saw him, and even if they did, they would not remember seeing him, because they were not attracted towards him. But let him enter the room feeling that he was magnetic and concentrating on this thought, others would feel his vibration. So remember the way you feel you can make others feel. This is the law. Make yourself a concentrated dynamo from which your thoughts vibrate to others. Then you are a power in the world. Cultivate the art of feeling, for as I said before you can only make others feel what you feel.

If you will study all of the great characters of history you will find that they were enthusiastic. First they were enthusiastic themselves, and then they could arouse others' enthusiasm. It is latent in everyone. It is a wonderful force when once aroused. All public men to be a success have to possess it. Cultivate it by concentration. Set aside some hour of the day, wherein to hold rapt converse with the soul. Meditate with sincere desire and contrite heart and you will be able to accomplish that which you have meditated on. This is the keynote of success.

"Think, speak and act just as you wish to be, And you will be that which you wish to be."

You are just what you think you are and not what you may appear to be. You may fool others but not yourself. You may control your life and actions just as you can control your hands. If you want to raise your hand you must first think of raising it. If you want to control your life you must first control your thinking. Easy to do, is it not? Yes it is, if you will but concentrate on what you think about.

For he only can
That says he will.

How can we secure concentration? To this question, the first and last answer must be: By interest and strong motive. The stronger the motive the greater the concentration.—Eustace Miller, M. D.

The Successful Lives Are the Concentrated Lives. The utterly helpless multitude that sooner or later have to be cared for by charity, are those that were never able to concentrate, and who have become the victims of negative ideas.

Train yourself so you will be able to centralize your thought and develop your brain power, and increase your mental energy, or you can be a slacker, a drifter, a quitter or a sleeper. It all depends on how you concentrate, or centralize your thoughts. Your thinking then becomes a fixed power and you do not waste time thinking about something that would not be good for you. You pick out the thoughts that will be the means of bringing you what you desire, and they become a material reality. Whatever we create in the thought world will some day materialize. That is the law. Don't forget this.

In the old days men drifted without concentration but this is a day of efficiency and therefore all of our efforts must be concentrated, if we are to win any success worth the name.

Why People Often Do Not Get What They Concentrate On. Because they sit down in hopeless despair and expect it to come to them. But if they will just reach out for it with their biggest effort they will find it is within their reach. No one limits us but ourselves. We are what we are today as the result of internal conditions. We can control the external conditions. They are subject to our will.

Through our concentration we can attract what we want, because we became enrapport with the Universal forces, from which we can get what we want.

You have watched races no doubt. They all line up together. Each has his mind set on getting to the goal before the others. This is one kind of concentration. A man starts to think on a certain subject. He has all kinds of thoughts come to him, but by concentration he shuts out all these but the one he has chosen. Concentration is just a case of willing to do a certain thing and doing it.

If you want to accomplish anything first put yourself in a concentrating, reposeful, receptive, acquiring frame of mind. In tackling unfamiliar work make haste slowly and deliberately and then you will secure that interior activity, which is never possible when you are in a hurry or under a strain. When you "think hard" or try to hurry results too quickly, you generally shut off the interior flow of thoughts and ideas. You have often no doubt tried hard to think of something but could not, but just as soon as you stopped trying to think of it, it came to you.

LESSON IX

Concentration Can Overcome Bad Habits

Habits make or break us to a far greater extent than we like to admit. Habit is both a powerful enemy and wonderful ally of concentration. You must learn to overcome habits which are injurious to concentration, and to cultivate those which increase it.

The large majority of people are controlled by their habits and are buffeted around by them like waves of the ocean tossing a piece of wood. They do things in a certain way because of the power of habit. They seldom ever think of concentrating on why they do them this or that way, or study to see if they could do them in a better way. Now my object in this chapter is to get you to concentrate on your habits so you can find out which are good and which are bad for you. You will find that by making a few needed changes you can make even those that are not good for you, of service; the good habits you can make much better.

The first thing I want you to realize is that all habits are governed consciously or unconsciously by the will. Most of us are forming new habits all the time. Very often, if you repeat something several times in the same way, you will have formed the habit of doing it that way. But the oftener you repeat it the stronger that habit grows and the more deeply it becomes embedded in your nature. After a habit has been in force for a long time, it becomes almost a part of you, and is therefore hard to overcome. But you can still break any habit by strong concentration on its opposite.

"All our life, so far as it has definite form, is but a mass of habits—practical, emotional, and intellectual—systematically organized, for our weal or woe, and bearing us irresistibly toward our destiny whatever the latter may be."

We are creatures of habits, "imitators and copiers of our past selves." We are liable to be "bent" or "curved" as we can bend a piece of paper, and each fold leaves a crease, which makes it easier to make the fold there the next time. "The intellect and will are spiritual functions; still they are immersed in matter, and to every movement of theirs, corresponds a movement in the brain, that is, in their material correlative." This is why habits of thought and habits of willing can be formed. All physical impressions are the carrying out of the actions of the will and intellect. Our nervous systems are what they are today, because of the way they have been exercised.

As we grow older most of us become more and more like automatic machines. The habits we have formed increase in strength. We work in our old characteristic way. Your associates learn to expect you to do things in a certain way. So you see that your habits make a great difference in your life, and as it is just about as easy to form good habits as it is bad, you should form only the former. No one but yourself is responsible for your habits. You are free to form the habits that you should and if everyone could realize the importance of forming the right kind of habits what a different world this would be. How much happier everyone would be. Then all instead of the few might win success.

Habits are formed more quickly when we are young, but if we have already passed the youthful plastic period the time to start to control our habits is right now, as we will never be any younger.

You will find the following maxims worth remembering.

First Maxim:

"We must make our nervous system our ally instead of our enemy."

Second Maxim:

"In the acquisition of a new habit as in the leaving off of an old one, we must take care to launch ourselves with as strong and decided an initiative as possible."

The man that is in the habit of doing the right thing from boyhood, has only good motives, so it is very important for you that you concentrate assiduously on the habits that reinforce good motives. Surround yourself with every aid you can. Don't play with fire by forming bad habits. Make a new beginning today. Study why you have been doing certain things. If they are not for your good, shun them henceforth. Don't give in to a single temptation for every time you do, you strengthen the chain of bad habits. Every time you keep a resolution you break the chain that enslaves you.

Third Maxim:

"Never allow an exception to occur till the new habit is securely rooted in your life." Here is the idea, you never want to give in, until the new habit is fixed else you undo all that has been accomplished by previous efforts. There are two opposing inclinations. One wants to be firm, and the other wants to give in. By your will you can become firm, through repetition. Fortify your will to be able to cope with any and all opposition.

Fourth Maxim:

"Seize the very first possible opportunity to act on every resolution you make, and on every emotional prompting you may experience in the direction of the habits you aspire to gain."

To make a resolve and not to keep it is of little value. So by all means keep every resolution you make, for you not only profit by the resolution, but it furnishes you with an exercise that causes the brain cells and physiological correlatives to form the habit of adjusting themselves to carry out resolutions. "A tendency to act, becomes effectively engrained in us in proportion to the uninterrupted frequency with which the actions actually occur, and the brain `grows' to their use. When a resolve or a fine glow of feeling is allowed to evaporate without bearing fruit, it is worse than a chance lost."

If you keep your resolutions you form a most valuable habit. If you break them you form a most dangerous one. So concentrate on keeping them, whether important or unimportant, and remember it is just as important for this purpose to keep the unimportant, for by so doing you are forming the habit.

Fifth Maxim:

"Keep the faculty of effort alive in you by a little gratuitous exercise every day."

The more we exercise the will, the better we can control our habits. "Every few days do something for no other reason than its difficulty, so that when the hour of dire need draws nigh, it may find you not unnerved or untrained to stand the test. Asceticism of this sort is like the insurance which a man pays on his house and goods. The tax does him no good at the time, and possibly may never bring him a return, but if the fire does come, his having paid it will be his salvation from ruin. So with the man who has daily insured himself to habits of concentrated attention, energetic volation, and self-denial in unnecessary things. "He will stand like a tower when everything rocks around him and his softer fellow-mortals are winnowed like chaff in the blast."

The young should be made to concentrate on their habits and be made to realize that if they don't they become walking bundles of injurious habits. Youth is the plastic state, and should be utilized in laying the foundation for a glorious future.

The great value of habit for good and evil cannot be overestimated. "Habit is the deepest law of human nature." No man is stronger than his habits, because his habits either build up his strength or decrease it.

Why We Are Creatures of Habits. Habits have often been called a labor-saying invention, because when they are formed they require less of both mental and material strength. The more deeply the habit becomes ingrained the more automatic it becomes. Therefore habit is an economizing tendency of our nature, for if it were not for habit we should have to be more watchful. We walk across a crowded street; the habit of stopping and looking prevents us from being hurt. The right kind of habits keeps us from making mistakes and mishaps. It is a well known fact that a chauffeur is not able to master his machine safely until he has trained his body in a habitual way. When an emergency comes he instantly knows what to do. Where safety depends on quickness the operator must work automatically. Habits mean less risk, less fatigue, and greater accuracy.

"You do not want to become a slave to habits of a trivial nature. For instance, Wagner required a certain costume before he could compose corresponding parts of his operas. Schiller could never write with ease unless there were rotten apples in the drawer of his desk from which he could now and then obtain an odor which seemed to him sweet. Gladstone had different desks for his different activities, so that when he worked on Homer he never sat among habitual accompaniments of his legislative labors."

In order to overcome undesirable habits, two things are necessary. You must have trained your will to do what you want it to do, and the stronger the will the easier it will be to break a habit. Then you must make a resolution to do just the opposite of what the habit is. Therefore one habit must replace another. If you have a strong will, you can tenaciously and persistently concentrate on removing the bad habit and in a very short time the good habit will gain the upper hand. I will bring this chapter to a close by giving Doctor Oppenheim's instructions for overcoming a habit:

"If you want to abolish a habit, and its accumulated circumstances as well, you must grapple with the matter as earnestly as you would with a physical enemy. You must go into the encounter with all tenacity of determination, with all fierceness of resolve—yea, even with a passion for success that may be called vindictive. No human enemy can be as insidious, so persevering, as unrelenting as an unfavorable habit. It never sleeps, it needs no rest.

"It is like a parasite that grows with the growth of the supporting body, and, like a parasite, it can best be killed by violent separation and crushing.

When life is stormy and all seems against us, that is when we often acquire wrong habits, and it is then, that we have to make a gigantic effort to think and speak as we should; and even though we may feel the very reverse at that moment the tiniest effort will be backed up by a tremendous Power and will lift us to a realization never felt before. It is not in the easy, contented moments of our life that we make our greatest progress, for then it requires, no special effort to keep in tune. But it is when we are in the midst of trials and misfortunes, when we think we are sinking, being overwhelmed, then it is important for us to realize that we are linked to a great Power and if we live as we should, there is nothing that can occur in life, which could permanently injure us, nothing can happen that should disturb us. So always remember you have within you unlimited power, ready to manifest itself in the form which fills our need at the moment. If, when we have something difficult to solve, we would be silent like the child, we can get the inspiration when it comes; we will know how to act, we will find there is no need to hurry or disturb ourselves, that it is always wiser to wait for guidance from within, than to act on impulse from Without.

LESSON X

Business Results Through Concentration

A successful business is not usually the result of chance. Neither is a failure the result of luck. Most failures could be determined in advance if the founders had been studied. It is not always possible to start a money-making business at the start. Usually a number of changes have to be made. Plans do not work out as their creators thought they would. They may have to be changed a little, broadened it may be, here and there, and as you broaden your business you broaden your power to achieve. You gain an intense and sustained desire to make your business a success.

When you start a business you may have but a vague notion of the way you will conduct it. You must fill in the details as you go along. You must concentrate on these details. As you straighten out one after another, others will require attention. In this way you cover the field of "the first endeavor" and new opportunities open up for you.

When you realize one desire, another comes. But if you do not fulfill the first desire, you will not the second. The person that does not carry his desires into action is only a dreamer. Desire is a great creative force, if it is pure, intense and sustained. It is our desires that keep stirring us up to action and they will strengthen and broaden you if you make them materialize.

Every man who achieves success deserves it. When he first started out he did not understand how to solve the problems that afterwards presented themselves, but he did each thing as it came up in the very best way that he could, and this developed his power of doing bigger things. We become masters of business by learning to do well whatever we attempt. The man that has a thorough knowledge of his business can of course direct it much more easily and skillfully than the man who lacks that knowledge. The skilled business director can sit in his private office and still know accurately what is actually being done. He knows what should be done in any given time and if it is not accomplished he knows that his employees are not turning out the work that they should. It is then easy to apply the remedy.

Business success depends on well-concentrated efforts. You must use every mental force you can master. The more these are used the more they increase. Therefore the more you accomplish today the more force you will have at your disposal with which to solve your problems tomorrow.

If you are working for someone else today and wish to start in a business for yourself, think over carefully what you would like to do. Then when you have resolved what you want to do, you will be drawn towards it. There is a law that opens the way to the fulfillment of your desires. Of course back of your desire you must put forward the necessary effort to carry out your purpose; you must use your power to put your desires into force. Once they are created and you keep up your determination to have them fulfilled you both consciously and unconsciously work toward their materialization. Set your heart on your purpose, concentrate your thought upon it, direct your efforts with all your intelligence and in due time you will realize your ambition.

Feel yourself a success, believe you are a success and thus put yourself in the attitude that demands recognition and the thought current draws to you what you need to make you a success. Don't be afraid of big undertakings. Go at them with grit, and pursue methods that you think will accomplish your purpose. You may not at first meet with entire success, but aim so high that if you fall a little short you will still have accomplished much.

What others have done you can do. You may even do what others have been unable to do. Always keep a strong desire to succeed in your mind. Be in love with your aim and work, and make them, as far as possible, square with the rule of the greatest good to the greatest number and your life cannot be a failure.

The successful business attitude must be cultivated to make the most out of your life, the attitude of expecting great things from both yourself and others. It alone will often cause men to make good; to measure up to the best that is in them.

It is not the spasmodic spurts that count on a long journey, but the steady efforts. Spurts fatigue and make it hard for you to continue.

Rely on your own opinion. It should be as good as anyone's else. When once you reach a conclusion abide by it. Let there be no doubt, or wavering in your judgment. If you are uncertain about every decision you make, you will be subject to harassing doubts and fears which will render your judgment of little value. The man that decides according to what he thinks right and who learns from every mistake acquires a well balanced mind that gets the best results. He gains the confidence of others. He is known as the man that knows what he wants, and not as one that is as changeable as the weather. The man of today wants to do business with the man that he can depend upon. Uncertainties in the business world are meeting with more disfavor. Reliable firms want to do business with men of known qualities, with men of firmness, judgment and reliability.

So if you wish to start in business for yourself your greatest asset, with the single exception of a sound physique, is that of a good reputation.

A successful business is not hard to build if we can concentrate all our mental forces upon it. It is the man that is unsettled because he does not know what he wants that goes to the wall. We hear persons say that business is trying on the nerves, but it is the unsettling elements of fret and worry and suspense that are nerve-exhausting and not the business. Executing one's plans may cause fatigue, enjoyment comes with rest. If there has not been any unnatural strain, the recuperative powers replace what energy has been lost.

By attending to each day's work properly you develop the capacity to do a greater work tomorrow. It is this gradual development that makes possible the carrying out of big plans. The man that figures out doing something each hour of the day gets somewhere. At the end of each day you should be a step nearer your aim. Keep the idea in mind, that you mean to go forward, that each day must mark an advance and forward you will go. You do not even have to know the exact direction so long as you are determined to find the way. But you must not turn back once you have started.

Even brilliant men's conceptions of the possibilities of their mental forces are so limited and below their real worth that they are far more likely to belittle their possibilities than they are to exaggerate them. You don't want to think that an aim is impossible because it has never been realized in the past. Every day someone is doing something that was never done before. We are pushing ahead faster. Formerly it took decades to build up a big business, but today it is only but a matter of years, sometimes of months.

Plan each day's activities carefully and you can reach any height you aim at. If each thing you do is done with concise and concentrated thought you will be able to turn out an excellent quality and a large quantity of work. Plan to do so much work during the day and you will be astonished to see how much more you will do, than on other days, when you had not decided on any certain amount. I have demonstrated that the average business working force could do the same amount of work in six hours that they now do in eight, without using up any more energy. Never start to accomplish anything in an indecisive, indefinite, uncertain way. Tackle everything with a positiveness and an earnestness that will concentrate your mind and attract the very best associated thoughts. You will in a short time find that you will have extra time for planning bigger things.

The natural leader always draws to himself, by the law of mental attraction, ideas in his chosen subject that have ever been conceived by others. This is of the greatest importance and help. If you are properly trained you benefit much by others' thoughts, and, providing you generate from within yourself something of value, they will benefit from yours. "We are heirs of all the ages," but we must know how to use our inheritance.

The confident, pushing, hopeful, determined man influences all with whom he associates, and inspires the same qualities in them. You feel that his is a safe example to follow and he rouses the same force within you that is pushing him onward and upward.

One seldom makes a success of anything that he goes at in a listless, spiritless way. To build up a business you must see it expanding in your mind before it actually takes tangible shape. Every great task that has ever been accomplished has first been merely a vision in the mind of its creator. Detail after detail has had to be worked out in his mind from his first faint idea of the enterprise. Finally a clear idea was formed and then the accomplishment, which was only the material result of the mental concept, followed.

The up-to-date business man is not content to build only for the present, but is planning ahead. If he does not he will fall behind his competitor, who is. What we are actually doing today was carefully thought out and planned by others in the past. All progressive businesses are conducted this way. That is why the young business man of today is likely to accomplish more in a few years than his father did in all his life. There is no reason why your work or business should fag you out. When it does there is something wrong. You are attracting forces and influence that you should not, because you are not in harmony with what you are doing. There is nothing so tiring as to try to do the work for which we are unfitted, both by temperament and training.

Each one should be engaged in a business that he loves; be should be furthering movements with which he is in sympathy. He will then only do his best work and take intense pleasure in his business. In this way, while constantly growing and developing his powers, he is at the same time rendering through his work, genuine and devoted service to humanity.

Business success is not the result of chance, but of scientific ideas and plans carried out by an aggressive and progressive management. Use your mental forces so that they will grow and develop. Remember that everything you do is the result of mental action, therefore you can completely control your every action. Nothing is impossible for you. Don't be afraid to tackle a difficult proposition. Your success will depend upon the use you make of your mind. This is capable of wonderful development. See that you make full use of it, and not only develop yourself but your associates. Try to broaden the visions of those with whom you come in contact and you will broaden your own outlook of life.

Are You Afraid of Responsibilities? In order for the individual soul to develop, you must have responsibilities. You must manifest the omnipotence of the law of supply. The whole world is your legitimate sphere of activity. How much of a conqueror are you? What have you done? Are you afraid of responsibility, or are you ever dodging, flinching, or side stepping it. If you are, you are not a Real Man. Your higher self never winces, so be a man and allow the powers of the higher self to manifest and you will find you have plenty of strength and you will feel better when you are tackling difficult propositions.

LESSON XI

Concentrate on Courage

Courage is the backbone of man. The man with courage has persistence. He states what he believes and puts it into execution. The courageous man has confidence. He draws to himself all the moral qualities and mental forces which go to make up a strong man. Whereas, the man without courage draws to himself all the qualities of a weak man, vacillation, doubt, hesitancy, and unsteadiness of purpose. You can therefore see the value of concentration on courage. It is a most vital element of success.

The lack of courage creates financial, as well as mental and moral difficulties. When a new problem comes, instead of looking upon it as something to be achieved, the man or woman without courage looks for reasons why it cannot be done and failure is naturally the almost inevitable result. This is a subject well worthy of your study. Look upon everything within your power as a possibility instead of as merely a probability and you will accomplish a great deal more, because by considering a thing as impossible, you immediately draw to yourself all the elements that contribute to failure. Lack of courage destroys your confidence in yourself. It destroys that forceful, resolute attitude so important to success.

The man without courage unconsciously draws to himself all that is contemptible, weakening, demoralizing and destructive. He then blames his luck when he does not secure the things he weakly desires. We must first have the courage to strongly desire something. A desire to be fulfilled must be backed by the strength of all our mental forces. Such a desire has enough commanding force to change all unfavorable conditions. The man with courage commands, whether be is on the battlefield or in business life.

What is courage? It is the Will To Do. It takes no more energy to be courageous than to be cowardly. It is a matter of the right training in the right way. Courage concentrates the mental forces on the task at hand. It then directs them thoughtfully, steadily, deliberately, while attracting all the forces of success, toward the desired end. Cowardice on the other hand, dissipates both our mental and moral forces, thereby inviting failure.

As we are creatures of habits, we should avoid persons that lack courage. They are easy to discover because of their habits of fear in attacking new problems. The man with courage is never afraid.

Start out today with the idea that there is no reason why you should not be courageous. If any fear-thoughts come to you cast them off as you would the deadly viper. Form the habit of never thinking of anything unfavorable to yourself or anyone else. In dealing with difficulties, new or old, hold ever the thought, "I am courageous." Whenever a doubt crosses the threshold of your mind, banish it. Remember, you as master of your mind control its every thought, and here is a good one to often affirm, "I have courage because I desire it; because I need it; because I use it and because I refuse to become such a weakling as cowardice produces."

There is no justification for the loss of courage. The evils by which you will almost certainly be overwhelmed without it are far greater than those which courage will help you to meet and overcome. Right, then, must be the moralist who says that the only thing to fear is fear.

Never let another's opinion affect you; he cannot tell what you are able to do; he does not know what you can do with your forces. The truth is you do not know yourself until you put yourself to the test. Therefore, how can someone else know? Never let anyone else put a valuation on you.

Almost all wonderful achievements have been accomplished after it had been "thoroughly" demonstrated that they were impossibilities. Once we understand the law, all things are possible. If they were impossibilities we could not conceive them.

Just the moment you allow someone to influence you against what you think is right, you lose that confidence in yourself that inspires courage and carries with it all the forces which courage creates. Just the moment you begin to swerve in your plan you begin to carry out another's thought and not your own. You become the directed and not the director. You forsake the courage and resolution of your own mind, and you therefore lack the very forces that you need to sustain and carry out your work. Instead of being self-reliant you become timid and this invites failure. When you permit yourself to be influenced from your plan by another, you are unable to judge as you should, because you have allowed another's influence to deprive you of your courage and determination without absorbing any of his in return so you are in much the same predicament, as you would be in if you turned over all your worldly possessions to another without getting "value received."

Concentrate on just the opposite of fear, want, poverty, sickness, etc. Never doubt your own ability. You have plenty, if you will just use it. A great many men are failures because they doubt their own capacity. Instead of building up strong mental forces which would be of the greatest use to them their fear thoughts tear them down. Fear paralyzes energy. It keeps us from attracting the forces that go to make up success. Fear is the worst enemy we have.

There are few people that really know that they can accomplish much. They desire the full extent of their powers, but alas, it is only occasionally that you find a man that is aware of the great possibilities within him. When you believe with all your mind and heart and soul that you can do something, you thereby develop the courage to steadily and confidently live up to that belief. You have now gone a long way towards accomplishing it. The chances are that there will be obstacles, big and little, in your way, but resolute courage will overcome them and nothing else will. Strong courage eliminates the injurious and opposing forces by summoning their masters, the yet stronger forces that will serve you.

Courage is yours for the asking. All you have to do is to believe in it, claim it and use it. To succeed in business believe that it will be successful, assert that it is successful, and work like a beaver to make it so. Difficulties soon melt away before the courageous. One man of courage can fire with his spirit a whole army of men, whether it be military or industrial, because courage, like cowardice, is contagious.

The man of courage overcomes the trials and temptations of life; he commands success; he renders sound judgment; he develops personal influence and a forceful character and often becomes the mentor of the community which he serves.

How to Overcome Depression and Melancholia. Both of the former are harmful and make you unhappy. These are states that can be quickly overcome through concentrating more closely on the higher self, for when you do you cut off the connection with the harmful force currents. You can also drive away moods by simply choosing and fully concentrating on an agreeable subject. Through will power and thought control we can accomplish anything we want to do. There is wonderful inherent power within us all, and there is never any sufficient cause for fear, except ignorance.

Every evil is but the product of ignorance, and everyone that possesses the power to think has the power to overcome ignorance and evil. The pain that we suffer from doing evil are but the lessons of experience, and the object of the pain is to make us realize our ignorance. When we become depressed It is evidence that our thought faculties are combining improperly and thereby attracting the wrong force-currents.

All that it is necessary to do is to exercise the will and concentrate upon happy subjects. I will only think of subjects worthy of my higher self and its powers.

LESSON XII

Concentrate on Wealth

It was never intended that man should be poor. When wealth is obtained under the proper conditions it broadens the life. Everything has its value. Everything has a good use and a bad use. The forces of mind like wealth can be directed either for good or evil. A little rest will re-create forces. Too much rest degenerates into laziness, and brainless, dreamy longings.

If you acquire wealth unjustly from others, you are misusing your forces; but if your wealth comes through the right sources you will be blessed. Through wealth we can do things to uplift ourselves and humanity.

Wealth is many persons' goal. It therefore stimulates their endeavor. They long for it in order to dress and live in such a way as to attract friends. Without friends they would not be so particular of their surroundings. The fact is the more attractive we make ourselves and our surroundings the more inspiring are their influences. It is not conducive to proper thought to be surrounded by conditions that are uncongenial and unpleasant.

So the first step toward acquiring wealth is to surround yourself with helpful influences; to claim for yourself an environment of culture, place yourself in it and be molded by its influences.

Most great men of all ages have been comparatively rich. They have made or inherited money. Without money they could not have accomplished what they did. The man engaged in physical drudgery is not likely to have the same high ideals as the man that can command comparative leisure.

Wealth is usually the fruit of achievement. It is not, however, altogether the result of being industrious. Thousands of persons work hard who never grow wealthy. Others with much less effort acquire wealth. Seeing possibilities is another step toward acquiring wealth. A man may be as industrious as he can possibly be, but if he does not use his mental forces he will be a laborer, to be directed by the man that uses to good advantage his mental forces.

No one can become wealthy in an ordinary lifetime, by mere savings from earnings. Many scrimp and economize all their lives; but by so doing waste all their vitality and energy. For example, I know a man that used to walk to work. It took him an hour to go and an hour to return. He could have taken a car and gone in twenty minutes. He saved ten cents a day but wasted an hour and a half. It was not a very profitable investment unless the time spent in physical exercise yielded him large returns in the way of health.

The same amount of time spent in concentrated effort to overcome his unfavorable business environment might have firmly planted his feet in the path of prosperity.

One of the big mistakes made by many persons of the present generation is that they associate with those who fail to call out or develop the best that is in them. When the social side of life is developed too exclusively, as it often is, and recreation or entertainment becomes the leading motive of a person's life, he acquires habits of extravagance instead of economy; habits of wasting his resources, physical, mental, moral and spiritual, instead of conserving them. He is, in consequence, lacking in proper motivation, his God-given powers and forces are undeveloped and he inevitably brings poor judgment to bear upon all the higher relationships of life, while, as to his financial fortunes, he is ever the leaner; often a parasite, and always, if opportunity affords, as heavy a consumer as he is a poor producer.

It seems a part of the tragedy of life that these persons have to be taught such painful lessons before they can understand the forces and laws that regulate life. Few profit by the mistakes of others. They must experience them for themselves and then apply the knowledge so gained in reconstructing their lives.

Any man that has ever amounted to anything has never done a great deal of detail work for long periods at any given time. He needs his time to reflect. He does not do his duties today in the same way as yesterday, but as the result of deliberate and concentrated effort, constantly tries to improve his methods.

The other day I attended a lecture on Prosperity. I knew the lecturer had been practically broke for ten years. I wanted to hear what he had to say. He spoke very well. He no doubt benefited some of his hearers, but he had not profited by his own teachings. I introduced myself and asked him if he believed in his maxims. He said he did. I asked him if they had made him prosperous. He said not exactly. I asked him why. He answered that he thought he was fated not to experience prosperity.

In half an hour I showed that man why poverty had always been his companion. He had dressed poorly. He held his lectures in poor surroundings. By his actions and beliefs he attracted poverty. He did not realize that his thoughts and his surroundings exercised an unfavorable influence. I said: "Thoughts are moving forces; great powers. Thoughts of wealth attract wealth. Therefore, if you desire wealth you must attract the forces that will help you to secure it. Your thoughts attract a similar kind of thoughts. If you hold thoughts of poverty you attract poverty. If you make up your mind you are going to be wealthy, you will instil this thought into all your mental forces, and you will at the same time use every external condition to help you."

Many persons are of the opinion that if you have money it is easy to make more money. But this is not necessarily true. Ninety per cent of the men that start in business fail. Money will not enable one to accumulate much more, unless he is trained to seek and use good opportunities for its investment. If he inherits money the chances are that he will lose it. While, if he has made it, he not only knows its value, but has developed the power to use it as well as to make more if he loses it.

Business success today depends on foresight, good judgment, grit, firm resolution and settled purpose. But never forget that thought is as real a force as electricity. Let your thoughts be such, that you will send out as good as you receive; if you do not, you are not enriching others, and therefore deserve not to be enriched.

The man that tries to get all he can from others for nothing becomes so selfish and mean that he does not even enjoy his acquisitions. We see examples of this every day. What we take from others, will in turn, be taken from us. All obligations have to be met fairly and squarely. We cannot reach perfection until we discharge every obligation of our lives. We all realize this, so why not willingly give a fair exchange for all that we receive?

Again I repeat that the first as well as the last step in acquiring wealth is to surround yourself with good influences—good thought, good health, good home and business environment and successful business associates. Cultivate, by every legitimate means, the acquaintance of men of big caliber. Bring your thought vibrations in regard to business into harmony with theirs. This will make your society not only agreeable, but sought after, and, when you have formed intimate friendships with clean, reputable men of wealth, entrust to them, for investment, your surplus earnings, however small, until you have developed the initiative and business acumen to successfully manage your own investments. By this time you will, through such associations, have found your place in life which, if you have rightly concentrated upon and used your opportunities, will not be among men of small parts. With a competence secured, you will take pleasure in using a part of it in making the road you traveled in reaching your position easier for those who follow you.

There is somewhere in every brain the energy that will get you out of that rut and put you far up on the mountain of success if you can only use the energy.

You know that gasoline in the engine of an automobile doesn't move the car until the spark comes to explode the gasoline.

So it is with the mind of man. We are not speaking now of men of great genius, but of average, able citizens.

Each one of them has in his brain the capacity to climb over the word impossible and get into the successful country beyond.

And hope, self-confidence and the determination to do something supply the spark that makes the energy work.

LESSON XIII

You can concentrate, But Will You?

All have the ability to concentrate, but will you? You can, but whether you will or not depends on you. It is one thing to be able to do something, and another thing to do it. There is far more ability not used than is used. Why do not more men of ability make something of themselves? There are comparatively few successful men but many ambitious ones. Why do not more get along? Cases may differ, but the fault is usually their own. They have had chances, perhaps better ones than some others that have made good.

What would you like to do, that you are not doing? If you think you should be "getting on" better, why don't you? Study yourself carefully. Learn your shortcomings. Sometimes only a mere trifle keeps one from branching out and becoming a success. Discover why you have not been making good—the cause of your failure. Have you been expecting someone to lead you, or to make a way for you? If you have, concentrate on a new line of thought.

There are two things absolutely necessary for success—energy and the will to succeed. Nothing can take the place of either of these. Most of us will not have an easy path to follow so don't expect to find one. The hard knocks develop our courage and moral stamina. The persons that live in an indolent and slipshod way never have any. They have never faced conditions and therefore don't know how. The world is no better for their living.

We must make favorable conditions and not expect them to shape themselves. It is not the man that says, "It can't be done," but the man that goes ahead in spite of adverse advice, and shows that "it can be done" that "gets there" today. "The Lord helps those that help themselves," is a true saying. We climb the road to success by overcoming obstacles. Stumbling blocks are but stepping stones for the man that says, "I can and I Will." When we see cripples, the deaf and dumb, the blind and those with other handicaps amounting to something in the world, the able-bodied man should feel ashamed of himself if he does not make good.

There is nothing that can resist the force of perseverance. The way ahead of all of us is not clear sailing, but all hard passages can be bridged, if you just think they can and concentrate on how to do it. But if you think the obstacles are unsurmountable, you will not of course try, and even if you do, it will be in only a half-hearted way—a way that accomplishes nothing.

Many men will not begin an undertaking unless they feel sure they will succeed in it. What a mistake! This would be right, if we were sure of what we could and could not do. But who knows? There may be an obstruction there now that might not be there next week. There may not be an obstruction there now that will be there next week. The trouble with most persons is that just as soon as they see their way blocked they lose courage. They forget that usually there is a way around the difficulty. It's up to you to find it. If you tackle something with little effort, when the conditions call for a big effort, you will of course not win. Tackle everything with a feeling that you will utilize all the power within you to make it a success. This is the kind of concentrated effort that succeeds.

Most people are beaten before they start. They think they are going to encounter obstacles, and they look for them instead of for means to overcome them. The result is that they increase their obstacles instead of diminishing them. Have you ever undertaken something that you thought would be hard, but afterwards found it to be easy? That is the way a great many times. The things that look difficult in advance turn out to be easy of conquest when once encountered. So start out on your journey with the idea that the road is going to be clear for you, and that if it is not you will clear the way. All men that have amounted to anything have cleared their way and they did not have the assistance that you will have today.

The one great keynote of success is to do whatever you have decided on. Don't be turned from your path, but resolve that you are going to accomplish what you set out to do. Don't be frightened at a few rebuffs, for they cannot stop the man that is determined—the man that knows in his heart that success is only bought by tremendous resolution, by concentrated and whole-hearted effort.

"He who has a firm will," says Goethe, "molds the world to himself."

"People do not lack strength," says Victor Hugo; "they lack Will."

It is not so much skill that wins victories as it is activity and great determination There is no such thing as failure for the man that does his best. No matter what you may be working at, at the present time, don't let this make you lose courage. The tides are continually changing, and tomorrow or some other day they will turn to your advantage if you are a willing and are an ambitious worker. There is nothing that develops you and increases your courage like work. If it were not for work how monotonous life would at last become!

So I say to the man that wants to advance, "Don't look upon your present position as your permanent one. Keep your eyes open, and add those qualities to your makeup that will assist you when your opportunity comes. Be ever alert and on the watch for opportunities. Remember, we attract what we set our minds on. If we look for opportunities, we find them.

If you are the man you should be, some one is looking for you to fill a responsible position. So when he finds you, don't let your attention wander. Give it all to him. Show that you can concentrate your powers, that you have the makeup of a real man. Show no signs of fear, uncertainty or doubt. The man that is sure of himself is bound to get to the front. No circumstances can prevent him.

LESSON XIV

The Art of Concentrating By Means of Practical Exercises

Select some thought, and see how long you can hold your mind on it. It is well to have a clock at first and keep track of the time. If you decide to think about health, you can get a great deal of good from your thinking besides developing concentration. Think of health as being the greatest blessing there is, in the world. Don't let any other thought drift in. Just the moment one starts to obtrude, make it get out.

Make it a daily habit of concentrating on this thought for, say, ten minutes. Practice until you can hold it to the exclusion of everything else. You will find it of the greatest value to centralize your thoughts on health. Regardless of your present condition, see yourself as you would like to be and be blind to everything else. You will find it hard at first to forget your ailments, if you have any, but after a short while you can shut out these negative thoughts and see yourself as you want to be. Each time you concentrate you form a more perfect image of health, and, as you come into its realization, you become healthy, strong and wholesome.

I want to impress upon your mind that the habit of forming mental images is of the greatest value. It has always been used by successful men of all ages, but few realize its full importance.

Do you know that you are continually acting according to the images you form? If you allow yourself to mould negative images you unconsciously build a negative disposition. You will think of poverty, weakness, disease, fear, etc. Just as surely as you think of these will your objective life express itself in a like way. Just what we think, we will manifest in the external world.

In deep concentration you become linked with the great creative spirit of the universe, and the creative energy then flows through you, vitalizing your creations into form. In deep concentration your mind becomes attuned with the infinite and registers the cosmic intelligence and receives its messages. You become so full of the cosmic energy that you are literally flooded with divine power. This is a most desired state. It is then we realize the advantages of being connected with the supra-consciousness.

The supra-consciousness registers the higher cosmic vibrations. It is often referred to as the wireless station, the message recorded coming from the universal mind.

There are very few that reach this stage of concentration. Very few even know that it is possible. They think concentration means limitation to one subject, but this deeper concentration that brings us into harmony with the Infinite is that which produces and maintains health.

When you have once come in contact with your supra-consciousness you become the controller of your human thoughts. That which comes to you is higher than human thoughts. It is often spoken of as Cosmic Consciousness. Once it is experienced it is never forgotten. Naturally it requires a good deal of training to reach this state, but once you do, it becomes easier each time to do, and in the course of time you can become possessed of power which was unknown to you before. You are able to direct the expression of almost Infinite Power while in this deeper state of concentration.

Exercises In Concentration. The rays of the sun, when focused upon an object by means of a sun glass, produce a heat many times greater than the scattered rays of the same source of light and heat. This is true of attention. Scatter it and you get but ordinary results. But center it upon one thing and you secure much better results. When you focus your attention upon an object your every action, voluntary and involuntary, is in the direction of attaining that object. If you will focus your energies upon a thing to the exclusion of everything else, you generate the force that can bring you what you want.

When you focus your thought, you increase its strength. The exercises that follow are tedious and monotonous, but useful. If you will persist in them you will find they are very valuable, as they increase your powers of concentration.

Before proceeding with the exercises I will answer a question that just comes to me. This person says after he works all day he is too tired to practice any exercise. But this is not true. We will say he comes home all tired out, eats his supper and sits down to rest. If his work has been mental, the thought which has been occupying his mind returns to him and this prevents him from securing the rest he needs.

It is an admitted fact that certain thoughts call into operation a certain set of brain cells; the other cells, of course, are not busy at that time and are rested. Now if you take up something that is just different from what you have been doing during the day, you will use the cells that have not done anything and give those that have had work to do a rest. So you should regulate the evenings that you have and call forth an entirely different line of thought so as not to use the cells which you have tired out during the day. If you will center your attention on a new thought, you relieve the old cells from vibrating with excitement and they get their needed rest. The other cells that have been idle all day want to work, and you will find you can enjoy your evenings while securing needed rest.

When once you have learned to master your thoughts, you will be able to change them just as easily as you change your clothes.

Remember, the real requisite of centering is to be able to shut out outside thoughts—anything foreign to the subject. Now, in order to control your intention first gain control over the body. This must be brought under direct control of the mind; the mind under the control of the will. Your will is strong enough to do anything you wish, but you must realize that it is. The mind can be greatly strengthened by being brought under the direct influence of the will. When the mind is properly strengthened by the impulse of the will it becomes a more powerful transmitter of thought, because it has more force.

The Best Time to Concentrate Is after reading something that is inspiring, as you are then mentally and spiritually exalted in the desired realm. Then is the time you are ready for deep concentration. If you are in your room first see that your windows are up and the air is good. Lie down flat on your bed without a pillow. See that every muscle is relaxed. Now breathe slowly, filling the lungs comfortably full of fresh air; hold this as long as you can without straining yourself; then exhale slowly. Exhale in an easy, rhythmic way. Breathe this way for five minutes, letting the Divine Breath flow through you, which will cleanse and rejuvenate every cell of brain and body.

You are then ready to proceed. Now think how quiet and relaxed you are. You can become enthusiastic over your condition. Just think of yourself as getting ready to receive knowledge that is far greater than you have ever received before. Now relax and let the spirit work in and through you and assist you to accomplish what you wish.

Don't let any doubts or fears enter. Just feel that what you wish is going to manifest. Just feel it already has, in reality it has, for just the minute you wish a thing to be done it manifests in the thought world. Whenever you concentrate just believe it is a success. Keep up this feeling and allow nothing to interfere and you will soon find you have become the master of concentration. You will find that this practice will be of wonderful value to you, and that rapidly you will be learning to accomplish anything that you undertake.

It will be necessary to first train the body to obey the commands of the mind. I want you to gain control of your muscular movements. The following exercise is especially good in assisting you to acquire perfect control of the muscles.

Exercise 1

Sit in a comfortable chair and see how still you can keep. This is not as easy as it seems. You will have to center your attention on sitting still. Watch and see that you are not making any involuntary muscular movements. By a little practice you will find you are able to sit still without a movement of the muscles for fifteen minutes. At first I advise sitting in a relaxed position for five minutes. After you are able to keep perfectly still, increase the time to ten minutes and then to fifteen. This is as long as it is necessary. But never strain yourself to keep still. You must be relaxed completely. You will find this habit of relaxing is very good.

Exercise 2

Sit in a chair with your head up and your chin out, shoulders back. Raise your right arm until it is on the level with your shoulder, pointing to your right. Look around, with head only, and fix your gaze on your fingers, and keep the arm perfectly still for one minute. Do the same exercise with left arm. When you are able to keep the arm perfectly steady, increase the time until you are able to do this five minutes with each arm. Turn the palm of the hand downward when it is outstretched, as this is the easiest position. If you will keep your eyes fixed on the tips of the fingers you will be able to tell if you are keeping your arm perfectly still.

Exercise 3

Fill a small glass full of water, and grasp it by the fingers; put the arm directly in front of you. Now fix the eyes upon the glass and try to keep the arm so steady that no movement will be noticeable. Do this first for one moment and then increase it to five. Do the exercise with first one arm and then the other.

Exercise 4

Watch yourself during the day and see that your muscles do not become tense or strained. See how easy and relaxed you can keep yourself. See how poised you can be at all times. Cultivate a self-poised manner, instead of a nervous, strained appearance. This mental feeling will improve your carriage and demeanor. Stop all useless gestures and movements of the body. These mean that you have not proper control over your body. After you have acquired this control, notice how "ill-at-ease" people are that have not gained this control. I have just been sizing up a salesman that has just left me. Part of his body kept moving all the time. I just felt like saying to him, "Do you know how much better appearance you would make if you would just learn to speak with your voice instead of trying to express what you say with your whole body?" Just watch those that interview you and see how they lack poise.

Get rid of any habit you have of twitching or jerking any part of your body. You will find you make many involuntary movements. You can quickly stop any of these by merely centering your attention on the thought, "I will not."

If you are in the habit of letting noises upset you, just exercise control; when the door slams, or something falls, etc., just think of these as exercises in self-control. You will find many exercises like this in your daily routine.

The purpose of the above exercises is to gain control over the involuntary muscular movement, making your actions entirely voluntary. The following exercises are arranged to bring your voluntary muscles under the control of the will, so that your mental forces may control your muscular movements.

Exercise 5

Move your chair up to a table, placing your hands upon it, clenching the fists, keeping the back of the hand on the table, the thumb doubled over the fingers. Now fix your gaze upon the fist for a while, then gradually extend the thumb, keeping your whole attention fixed upon the act, just as if it was a matter of great importance. Then gradually extend your first finger, then your second and so on until you open the rest. Then reverse the process, closing first the last one opened and then the rest, and finally you will have the fist again in the original position with the thumb closed over the finger. Do this exercise with the left hand. Keep up this exercise first with one hand and then the other until you have done it five times with each hand. In a few days you can increase it to ten times.

The chances are that the above exercises will at first make you "tired," but it is important for you to practice these monotonous exercises so you can train your attention. It also gives you control over your muscular movement. The attention, of course, must be kept closely on each movement of the hand; if it is not, you of course lose the value of the exercise.

Exercise 6

Put the right hand on knee, both fingers and thumb closed, except the first finger, which points out in front of you. Then move the finger slowly from side to side, keeping the attention fixed upon the end of the finger. You can make up a variety of exercises like these. It is good training to plan out different ones. The main point you should keep in mind is that the exercise should be simple and that the attention should be firmly fixed upon the moving part of the body. You will find your attention will not want to be controlled and will try to drift to something more interesting. This is just where these exercises are of value, and you must control your attention and see it is held in the right place and does not wander away.

You may think these exercises very simple and of no value, but I promise you in a short time you will notice that you have a much better control over your muscular movements, carriage and demeanor, and you will find that you have greatly improved your power of attention, and can center your thoughts on what you do, which of course will be very valuable.

No matter what you may be doing, imagine that it is your chief object in life. Imagine you are not interested in anything else in the world but what you are doing. Do not let your attention get away from the work you are at. Your attention will no doubt be rebellious, but control it and do not let it control you. When once you conquer the rebellious attention you have achieved a greater victory than you can realize at the time. Many times afterwards you will be thankful you have learned to concentrate your closest attention upon the object at hand.

Let no day go by without practicing concentrating on some familiar object that is uninteresting. Never choose an interesting object, as it requires less attention. The less interesting it is the better exercise will it be. After a little practice you will find you can center your attention on uninteresting subjects at will.

The person that can concentrate can gain full control over his body and mind and be the master of his inclinations; not their slave. When you can control yourself you can control others. You can develop a Will that will make you a giant compared with the man that lacks Will Power. Try out your Will Power in different ways until you have it under such control that just as soon as you decide to do a thing you go ahead and do it. Never be satisfied with the "I did fairly well" spirit, but put forward your best efforts. Be satisfied with nothing else. When you have gained this you are the man you were intended to be.

Exercise 7

Concentration Increases the Sense of Smell. When you take a walk, or drive in the country, or pass a flower garden, concentrate on the odor of flowers and plants. See how many different kinds you can detect. Then choose one particular kind and try to sense only this. You will find that this strongly intensifies the sense of smell. This differentiation requires, however, a peculiarly attentive attitude. When sense of smell is being developed, you should not only shut out from the mind every thought but that of odor, but you should also shut out cognizance of every odor save that upon which your mind, for the time, is concentrated.

You call find plenty of opportunity for exercises for developing the sense of smell. When you are out in the air, be on the alert for the different odors. You will find the air laden with all kinds, but let your concentration upon the one selected be such that a scent of its fragrance in after years will vividly recall the circumstances of this exercise.

The object of these exercises is to develop concentrated attention, and you will find that you can, through their practice, control your mind and direct your thoughts just the same as you can your arm.

Exercise 8

Concentration on the Within. Lie down and thoroughly relax your muscles. Concentrate on the beating of your heart. Do not pay any attention to anything else. Think how this great organ is pumping the blood to every part of the body; try to actually picture the blood leaving the great reservoir and going in one stream right down to the toes. Picture another going down the arms to the tips of the fingers. After a little practice you can actually feel the blood passing through your system.

If, at any time, you feel weak in any part of the body, will that an extra supply of blood shall go there. For instance, if your eyes feel tired, picture the blood coming from the heart, passing up through the head and out to the eyes. You can wonderfully increase your strength by this exercise. Men have been able to gain such control over the heart that they have actually stopped it from beating for five minutes. This, however, is not without danger, and is not to be practiced by the novice.

I have found the following a very helpful exercise to take just before going to bed and on rising in the morning: Say to yourself, "Every cell in my body thrills with life; every part of my body is strong and healthy." I have known a number of people to greatly improve their health in this way. You become what you picture yourself to be. If your mind thinks of sickness in connection with self you will be sick. If you imagine yourself in strong, vigorous health, the image will be realized. You will be healthy.

Exercise 9

Concentrating on Sleep. What is known as the water method is, although very simple, very effective in inducing sleep.

Put a full glass of clear water on a table in your sleeping room. Sit in a chair beside the table and gaze into the glass of water and think how calm it is. Then picture yourself , getting into just as calm a state. In a short time you will find the nerves becoming quiet and you will be able to go to sleep. Sometimes it is good to picture yourself becoming drowsy to induce sleep, and, again, the most persistent insomnia has been overcome by one thinking of himself as some inanimate object—for instance, a hollow log in the depths of the cool, quiet forest.

Those who are troubled with insomnia will find these sleep exercises that quiet the nerves very effective. Just keep the idea in your mind that there is no difficulty in going to sleep; banish all fear of insomnia. Practice these exercises and you will sleep.

By this time you should have awakened to the possibilities of concentration and have become aware of the important part it plays in your life.

Exercise 10

Concentration Will Save Energy and Appearance. Watch yourself and see if you are not in the habit of moving your hands, thumping something with your fingers or twirling your mustache. Some have the habit of keeping their feet going, as, for instance, tapping them on the floor. Practice standing before a mirror and see if you are in the habit of frowning or causing wrinkles to appear in the forehead. Watch others and see how they needlessly twist their faces in talking. Any movement of the face that causes the skin to wrinkle will eventually cause a permanent wrinkle. As the face is like a piece of silk, you can make a fold in it a number of times and it will straighten out of itself, but, if you continue to make a fold in it, it will in time be impossible to remove it.

By Concentration You Can Stop the Worry Habit. If you are in the habit of worrying over the merest trifles, just concentrate on this a few minutes and see bow needless it is; if you are also in the habit of becoming irritable or nervous at the least little thing, check yourself instantly when you feel yourself becoming so; start to breathe deeply; say, "I will not be so weak; I am master of myself," and you will quickly overcome your condition.

Exercise 11

By Concentration You Can Control Your Temper. If you are one of those that flare up at the slightest "provocation" and never try to control yourself, just think this over a minute. Does it do you any good? Do you gain anything by it? Doesn't it put you out of poise for some time? Don't you know that this grows on you and will eventually make you despised by all that have any dealings with you? Everyone makes mistakes and, instead of becoming angry at their perpetrators, just say to them, "Be more careful next time." This thought will be impressed on them and they will be more careful. But, if you continually complain about their making a mistake, the thought of a mistake is impressed on them and they will be more likely to make mistakes in the future. All lack of self-control can be conquered if you will but learn to concentrate.

Many of you that read this may think you are not guilty of either of these faults, but if you will carefully watch yourself you will probably find that you are, and, if so, you will be greatly helped by repeating this affirmation each morning:

"I am going to try today not to make a useless gesture or to worry over trifles, or become nervous or irritable. I intend to be calm, and, no difference what may be the circumstances, I will control myself. Henceforth I resolve to be free from all signs that show lack of self-control."

At night quickly review your actions during the day and see how fully you realized your aim. At first you will, of course, have to plead guilty of violation a few times, but keep on, and you will soon find that you can live up to your ideal. After you have once gained self-control, however, don't relinquish it. For some time it will still be necessary to repeat the affirmation in the morning and square your conduct with it in the evening. Keep up the good work until, at last, the habit of self-control is so firmly fixed that you could not break it even though you tried.

I have had many persons tell me that this affirmation and daily review made a wonderful difference in their lives. You, too, will notice the difference if you live up to these instructions.

Exercise 12.

Practice Talking Before a Glass. Make two marks on your mirror on a level with your eyes, and think of them as two human eyes looking into yours. Your eyes will probably blink a little at first. Do not move your head, but stand erect. Concentrate all your thoughts on keeping your head perfectly still. Do not let another thought come into your mind. Then, still keeping the head, eyes and body still, think that you look like a reliable man or woman should; like a person that anyone would have confidence in. Do not let your appearance be such as to justify the remark, "I don't like his appearance. I don't believe he can be trusted."

While standing before the mirror practice deep breathing. See that there is plenty of fresh air in the room, and that you are literally feasting on it. You will find that, as it permeates every cell, your timidity will disappear. It has been replaced by a sense of peace and power.

The one that stands up like a man and has control over the muscles of his face and eyes always commands attention. In his conversation, he can better impress those with whom he comes in contact. He acquires a feeling of calmness and strength that causes opposition to melt away before it.

Three minutes a day is long enough for the practice of this exercise.

Look at the clock before you commence the exercise, and if you find you can prolong the exercise for more than five minutes do so. The next day sit in a chair and, without looking at the picture, concentrate on it and see if you cannot think of additional details concerning it. The chances are you will be able to think of many more. It might be well for you to write down all you thought of the first day, and then add to the list each new discovery. You will find that this is a very excellent exercise in concentration.

Exercise 13

The Control of Sensations. Think how you would feel if you were cool; then how you would feel if you were cold; again, how you would feel if it were freezing. In this state you would be shivering all over. Now think of just the opposite conditions; construct such a vivid image of heat that you are able to experience the sensation of heat even in the coldest atmosphere. It is possible to train your imagination until you do this, and it can then be turned to practical account in making undesirable conditions bearable.

You can think of many very good exercises like this. For instance, if you feel yourself getting hungry or thirsty and for any reason you do not wish to eat, do not think of how hungry or thirsty you are, but just visualize yourself as finishing a hearty meal. Again, when you experience pain, do not increase it by thinking about it, but do something to divert your attention, and the pain will seem to decrease. If you will start practicing along this line systematically you will soon gain a wonderful control over the things that affect your physical comfort.

Exercise 14

The Eastern Way of Concentrating. Sit in a chair with a high back in upright position. Press one finger against the right nostril. Now take a long, deep breath, drawing the breath in gently as you count ten; then expel the breath through the right nostril as you count ten. Repeat this exercise with the opposite nostril. This exercise should be done at least twenty times at each sitting.

Exercise 15

Controlling Desires. Desire, which is one of the hardest forces to control, will furnish you with excellent exercises in concentration. It seems natural to want to tell others what you know; but, by learning to control these desires, you can wonderfully strengthen your powers of concentration. Remember, you have all you can do to attend to your own business. Do not waste your time in thinking of others or in gossiping about them.

If, from your own observation, you learn something about another person that is detrimental, keep it to yourself. Your opinion may afterwards turn out to be wrong anyway, but whether right or wrong, you have strengthened your will by controlling your desire to communicate your views.

If you hear good news resist the desire to tell it to the first person you meet and you will be benefited thereby. It will require the concentration of all your powers of resistance to prohibit the desire to tell. After you feel that you have complete control over your desires you can then tell your news. But you must be able to suppress the desire to communicate the news until you are fully ready to tell it. Persons that do not possess this power of control over desires are apt to tell things that they should not, thereby often involving both themselves and others in needless trouble.

If you are in the habit of getting excited when you hear unpleasant news, just control yourself and receive it without any exclamation of surprise. Say to yourself, "Nothing is going to cause me to lose my self-control. You will find from experience that this self-control will be worth much to you in business. You will be looked upon as a cool-headed business man, and this in time becomes a valuable business asset. Of course, circumstances alter cases. At times it is necessary to become enthused. But be ever on the lookout for opportunities for the practice of self-control. "He that ruleth his spirit is greater than he that ruleth a city."

Exercise 16

When You Read. No one can think without first concentrating his thoughts on the subject in hand. Every man and woman should train himself to think clearly. An excellent exercise is to read some short story and then write just an abridged statement. Read an article in a newspaper, and see in how few words you can express it. Reading an article to get only the essentials requires the closest concentration. If you are unable to write out what you read, you will know you are weak in concentration. Instead of writing it out you can express it orally if you wish. Go to your room and deliver it as if you were talking to some one. You will find exercises like this of the greatest value in developing concentration and learning to think.

After you have practiced a number of these simple exercises read a book for twenty minutes and then write down what you have read. The chances are that at first you will not remember very many details, but with a little practice you will be able to write a very good account of what you have read. The closer the concentration the more accurate the account will be.

It is a good idea when time is limited to read only a short sentence and then try to write it down word for word. When you are able to do this, read two or more sentences and treat similarly. The practice will produce very good results if you keep it up until the habit is fixed.

If you will just utilize your spare time in practicing exercises like those suggested you can gain wonderful powers of concentration. You will find that in order to remember every word in a sentence you must keep out every thought but that which you wish to remember, and this power of inhibition alone will more than compensate for the trouble of the exercise. Of course, success in all of the above depends largely upon cultivating, through the closest concentration, the power to image or picture what you read; upon the power, as one writer expresses it, of letting the mountains of which we hear loom before us and the rivers of which we read roll at our feet.

Exercise 17

Concentration Overcomes Bad Habits. If you have a habit that you want to get rid of, shut your eyes and imagine that your real self is standing before you. Now try the power of affirmation; say to yourself, "You are not a weakling; you can stop this habit if you want to. This habit is bad and you want to break it." Just imagine that you are some one else giving this advice. This is very valuable practice. You, in time, see yourself as others see you. The habit loses its power over you and you are free.

If you will just form the mental image of controlling yourself as another person might, you will take a delight in breaking bad habits. I have known a number of men to break themselves of drinking in this way.

Exercise 18

Watch Concentration. Sit in a chair and place a clock with a second hand on the table. Follow the second hand with your eyes as it goes around. Keep this up for five minutes, thinking of nothing else but the second hand, This is a very good exercise when you only have a few minutes to spare, if you are able to keep every other thought in the stream of consciousness subordinate to it. As there is little that is particularly interesting about the second hand, it is hard to do this, but in the extra effort of will power required to make it successful lies its value. Always try to keep as still as possible during these exercises.

In this way you can gain control over nerves and this quieting effect is very good for them.

Exercise 19

Faith Concentration. A belief in the power to concentrate is of course very important. I purposely did not put this exercise in the beginning where it naturally belongs because I wanted you to know that you could learn to concentrate. If you have practiced the above exercises you have now developed this concentration power to a considerable extent and therefore you have faith in the power of concentration, but you can still become a much stronger believer in it.

We will say that you have some desire or wish you want fulfilled, or that you need some special advice. You first clearly picture what is wanted and then you concentrate on getting it. Have absolute faith that your desires will be realized. Believe that it will according to your belief be fulfilled. Never, at this time, attempt to analyze the belief. You don't care anything about the whys and wherefores. You want to gain the thing you desire, and if you concentrate on it in the right way you will get it.

A Caution. Never think you will not succeed, but picture what is wanted as already yours, and yours it surely will be.

Self-Distrust. Do you ever feel distrust in yourself? If You do, just ask yourself, which self do I mistrust? Then say: my higher self cannot be affected. Then think of the wonderful powers of the higher self. There is a way to overcome all difficulties, and it is a delight for the human soul to do so. Instead of wasting precious thought-force by dreading or fearing a disagreeable interview or event, instead devote the time and concentrated thought in how to make the best of the interview or event and you will find that it will not be as unpleasant as you thought it would be. Most of our troubles are but imaginary, and it is the mental habit of so dreading them that really acts as a magnet in attracting those that really do come. Your evil circumstances are created or attracted by your own negative, fears and wrong thoughts, and are a means of teaching you to triumph over all evils, by discovering that which is inherent within yourself.

You will find it helpful in overcoming self-distrust, to stop and think, why you are, concentrating your forces, and by so doing you become more closely attached to the higher self, which never distrusts.

LESSON XV

Concentrate So You will not Forget

A man forgets because he does not concentrate his mind on his purpose, especially at the moment he conceives it. We remember only that which makes a deep impression, hence we must first deepen our impressions by associating in our minds certain ideas that are related to them.

We will say a wife gives her husband a letter to mail. He does not think about it, but automatically puts it in his pocket and forgets all about it. When the letter was given to him had he said to himself, "I will mail this letter. The box is at the next corner and when I pass it I must drop this letter," it would have enabled him to recall the letter the instant he reached the mail box.

The same rule holds good in regard to more important things. For example, if you are instructed to drop in and see Mr. Smith while out to luncheon today, you will not forget it, if, at the moment the instruction is given, you say to yourself something similar to the following:

"When I get to the corner of Blank street, on my way to luncheon, I shall turn to the right and call on Mr. Smith." In this way the impression is made, the connection established and the sight of the associated object recalls the errand.

The important thing to do is to deepen the impression at the very moment it enters your mind. This is made possible, not only by concentrating the mind upon the idea itself, but by surrounding it with all possible association of ideas, so that each one will reinforce the others.

The mind is governed by laws of association, such as the law that ideas which enter the mind at the same time emerge at the same time, one assisting in recalling the others.

The reason why people cannot remember what they want to is that they have not concentrated their minds sufficiently on their purpose at the moment when it was formed.

You can train yourself to remember in this way by the concentration of the attention on your purpose, in accordance with the laws of association.

When once you form this habit, the attention is easily centered and the memory easily trained. Then your memory, instead of failing you at crucial moments, becomes a valuable asset in your every-day work.

Exercise in Memory Concentration. Select some picture; put it on a table and then look at it for two minutes. Concentrate your attention on this picture, observe every detail; then shut your eyes and see how much you can recall about it. Think of what the picture represents; whether it is a good subject; whether it looks natural. Think of objects in foreground, middle ground, background; of details of color and form. Now open your eyes and hold yourself rigidly to the correction of each and every mistake. Close eyes again and notice how much more accurate your picture is. Practice until your mental image corresponds in every particular to the original.

Nature is a Wonderful Instructor. But there are very few who realize that when we get in touch with nature we discover ourselves. That by listening to her voice, with that curious, inner sense of ours, we learn the oneness of life and wake up to our own latent powers.

Few realize that the simple act of listening and concentrating is our best interior power, for it brings us into close contact with the highest, just as our other senses bring us into touch with the coarser side of human nature. The closer we live to nature the more developed is this sense. "So called" civilization has over developed our other senses at the expense of this one.

Children unconsciously realize the value of concentration—for instance: When a Child has a difficult problem to solve, and gets to some knotty point which he finds himself mentally unable to do—though he tries his hardest—he will pause and keep quite still, leaning on his elbow, apparently listening; then you will see, if you are watching, sudden illumination come and he goes on happily and accomplishes his task. A child instinctively but unconsciously knows when he needs help, he must be quiet and concentrate.

All great people concentrate and owe their success to it. The doctor thinks over the symptoms of his patient, waits, listens for the inspiration, though quite unconscious, perhaps, of doing so. The one who diagnoses in this way seldom makes mistakes. An author thinks his plot, holds it in his mind, and then waits, and illumination comes. If you want to be able to solve difficult problems you must learn to do the same.

LESSON XVI

How Concentration Can Fulfill Your Desire

"It is a spiritual law that the desire to do necessarily implies the ability to do."

You have all read of "Aladdin's Lamp," which accomplished such wonderful things. This, of course, is only a fairy story, but it illustrates the fact that man has within him the power, if he is able to use it, to gratify his every wish.

If you are unable to satisfy your deepest longings it is time you learned how to use your God-given powers. You will soon be conscious that you have latent powers within capable when once developed of revealing to you priceless knowledge and unlimited possibilities of success.

Man should have plenty of everything and not merely substance to live on as so many have. All natural desires can be realized. It would be wrong for the Infinite to create wants that could not be supplied. Man's very soul is in his power to think, and it, therefore, is the essence of all created things. Every instinct of man leads to thought, and in every thought there is great possibility because true thought development, when allied to those mysterious powers which perhaps transcend it, has been the cause of all the world's true progress.

In the silence we become conscious of "that something" which transcends thought and which uses thought as a medium for expression. Many have glimpses of "that something," but few ever reach the state where the mind is steady enough to fathom these depths. Silent, concentrated thought is more potent than spoken words, for speech distracts from the focusing power of the mind by drawing more and more attention to the without.

Man must learn more and more to depend on himself; to seek more for the Infinite within. It is from this source alone that he ever gains the power to solve his practical difficulties. No one should give up when there is always the resources of Infinity. The cause of failure is that men search in the wrong direction for success, because they are not conscious of their real powers that when used are capable of guiding them.

The Infinite within is foreign to those persons who go through life without developing their spiritual powers. But the Infinite helps only he who helps himself. There is no such thing as a Special "Providence." Man will not receive help from the Infinite except to the extent that he believes and hopes and prays for help from this great source.

Concentrate on What You Want and Get It. The weakling is controlled by conditions. The strong man controls conditions. You can be either the conqueror or the conquered. By the law of concentration you can achieve your heart's desire. This law is so powerful that that which at first seems impossible becomes attainable.

By this law what you at first see as a dream becomes a reality.

Remember that the first step in concentration is to form a Mental Image of what you wish to accomplish. This image becomes a thought-seed that attracts thoughts of a similar nature. Around this thought, when it is once planted in the imagination or creative region of the mind, you group or build associated thoughts which continue to grow as long as your desire is keen enough to compel close concentration.

Form the habit of thinking of something you wish to accomplish for five minutes each day. Shut every other thought out of consciousness. Be confident that you will succeed; make up your mind that all obstacles that are in your way will be overcome and you can rise above any environment.

You do this by utilizing the natural laws of the thought world which are all powerful.

A great aid in the development of concentration is to write out your thoughts on that which lies nearest your heart and to continue, little by little, to add to it until you have as nearly as possible exhausted the subject.

You will find that each day as you focus your forces on this thought at the center of the stream of consciousness, new plans, ideas and methods will flash into your mind. There is a law of attraction that will help you accomplish your purpose. An advertiser, for instance, gets to thinking along a certain line. He has formed his own ideas, but he wants to know what others think. He starts out to seek ideas and he soon finds plenty of books, plans, designs, etc., on the subject, although when he started he was not aware of their existence.

The same thing is true in all lines. We can attract those things that will help us. Very often we seem to receive help in a miraculous way. It may be slow in coming, but once the silent unseen forces are put into operation, they will bring results so long as we do our part. They are ever present and ready to aid those who care to use them. By forming a strong mental image of your desire, you plant the thought-seed which begins working in your interest and, in time, that desire, if in harmony with your higher nature, will materialize.

It may seem that it would be unnecessary to caution you to concentrate only upon achievement that will be good for you and work no harm to another, but there are many who forget others and their rights, in their anxiety to achieve success. All good things are possible for you to have, but only as you bring your forces into harmony with that law that requires that we mete out justice to fellow travelers as we journey along life's road. So first think over the thing wanted and if it would be good for you to have; say, "I want to do this; I am going to work to secure it. The way will be open for me."

If you fully grasp mentally the thought of success and hold it in mind each day, you gradually make a pattern or mold which in time will materialize. But by all means keep free from doubt and fear, the destructive forces. Never allow these to become associated with your thoughts.

At last you will create the desired conditions and receive help in many unlooked-for ways that will lift you out of the undesired environment. Life will then seem very different to you, for you will have found happiness through awakening within yourself the power to become the master of circumstances instead of their slave.

To the beginner in this line of thought some of the things stated in this book may sound strange, even absurd, but, instead of condemning them, give them a trial. You will find they will work out.The inventor has to work out his idea mentally before he produces it materially. The architect first sees the mental picture of the house he is to plan and from this works out the one we see. Every object, every enterprise, must first be mentally created.

I know a man that started in business with thirteen cents and not a dollar's worth of credit. In ten years he has built up a large and profitable business. He attributes his success to two things—belief that he would succeed and hard work. There were times when it did not look like he could weather the storm. He was being pressed by his creditors who considered him bankrupt. They would have taken fifty cents on the dollar for his notes and considered themselves lucky. But by keeping up a bold front he got an extension of time when needed. When absolutely necessary for him to raise a certain sum at a certain time he always did it. When he had heavy bills to meet he would make up his mind that certain people that owed him would pay by a certain date and they always did. Sometimes he would not receive their check until the last mail of the day of the extension, and I have known him to send out a check with the prospect of receiving a check from one of his customers the following day. He would have no reason other than his belief in the power of affecting the mind of another by concentration of thought for expecting that check, but rarely has he been disappointed.

Just put forth the necessary concentrated effort and you will be wonderfully helped from sources unknown to you.

Remember the mystical words of Jesus, the Master: "Whatsoever thing ye desire when ye pray, pray as if ye had already received and ye shall have."

LESSON XVII

Ideals Developed by Concentration

Through our paltry stir and strife, Glows the wished Ideal, And longing molds in clay, what life Carves in the marble real.—Lowell.

We often hear people spoken of as idealists. The fact is we are all idealists to a certain extent, and upon the ideals we picture depends our ultimate success. You must have the mental image if you are to produce the material thing. Everything is first created in the mind. When you control your thoughts you become a creator. You receive divine ideas and shape them to your individual needs. All things of this world are to you just what you think they are. Your happiness and success depend upon your ideals.

You are responsible for every condition you go through, either consciously or unconsciously. The next step you take determines the succeeding step. Remember this; it is a valuable lesson. By concentrating on each step as you go along, you can save a lot of waste steps and will be able to choose a straight path instead of a roundabout road.

Concentrate Upon Your Ideals and They Will Become Material Actualities. Through concentration we work out our ideals in physical life. Your future depends upon the ideals you are forming now. Your past ideals are determining your present. Therefore, if you want a bright future, you must begin to prepare for it today.

If persons could only realize that they can only injure themselves, that when they are apparently injuring others they are really injuring themselves, what a different world this would be!

We say a man is as changeable as the weather. What is meant is his ideals change. Every time you change your ideal you think differently. You become like a rudderless boat on an ocean. Therefore realize the importance of holding to your ideal until it becomes a reality.

You get up in the morning determined that nothing will make you lose your temper. This is your ideal of a person of real strength and poise. Something takes place that upsets you completely and you lose your temper. For the time being you forget your ideal. If you had just thought a second of what a well-poised person implies you would not have become angry. You lose your poise when you forget your ideal. Each time we allow our ideals to be shattered we also weaken our will-power. Holding to your ideals develops will-power. Don't forget this.

Why do so many men fail? Because they don't hold to their ideal until it becomes a mental habit. When they concentrate on it to the exclusion of all other things it becomes a reality.

"I am that which I think myself to be."

Ideals are reflected to us from the unseen spirit. The laws of matter and spirit are not the same. One can be broken, but not the other. To the extent that ideals are kept is your future assured.

It was never intended that man should suffer. He has brought it upon himself by disobeying the laws of nature. He knows them so cannot plead ignorance. Why does he break them? Because he does not pay attention to those ideals flashed to him from the Infinite Spirit.

Life is but one continuous unfoldment, and you can be happy every step of the way or miserable, as you please; it all depends upon how we entertain those silent whisperings that come from we know not where. We cannot hear them with mortal ear, but from the silence they come as if they were dreams, not to you or me alone, but to everyone. In this way the grandest thoughts come to us, to use or abuse. So search not in treasured volumes for noble thoughts, but within, and bright and glowing vision will come to be realized now and hereafter.

You must give some hours to concentrated, consistent, persistent thought. You must study yourself and your weaknesses.

No man gets over a fence by wishing himself on the other side. He must climb.

No man gets out of the rut of dull, tiresome, monotonous life by merely wishing himself out of the rut. He must climb.

If you are standing still, or going backward, there is something wrong. You are the man to find out what is wrong.

Don't think that you are neglected, or not understood, or not appreciated.

Such thoughts are the thoughts of failure.

Think hard about the fact that men who have got what you envy got it by working for it.

Don't pity yourself, criticise yourself.

You know that the only thing in the world that you have got to count upon is yourself.

LESSON XVIII

Mental Control Through Creation

I attended a banquet of inventors recently. Each inventor gave a short talk on something he thought would be accomplished in the future. Many very much needed things were spoken of. One inventor spoke of the possibilities of wireless telephone. Distance, he said, would shortly be annihilated. He thought we would soon be able to talk to the man in the submarine forty fathoms below the surface and a thousand miles away. When he got through he asked if there were any that doubted what he said. No one spoke up. This was not a case of tactful politeness, as inventors like to argue, but a case where no one present really doubted that the inventor's vision would, in the future, materialize.

These shrewd men, some real geniuses, all thought we would in time be able to talk to those a thousand miles away without media. Now, if we can make an instrument so wonderful that we can send wireless messages a thousand miles, is there any reason why we should not through mental control transmit messages from one person to another? The wireless message should not be as easy to send as the projected thought.

The day will come when all business will employ highly developed persons to send out influences. These influences will be so dominating that employes will be partly controlled by them and so you will profit more and more by your mental powers and depend on them to draw to you all forces of a helpful nature. You will be constantly sending out suggestions to your employes and friends. They will receive these unconsciously, but in case yours is the stronger personality they will carry them out the same as if you had spoken them.

This is being done even today. A finely organized company secures the combined effort of all its men. They may be each doing a different kind of work, but all work to bring about the very best results. The whole atmosphere is impregnated with a high standard of workmanship. Everyone feels he must do his best. He could not be in such surroundings and be satisfied to do anything but his best work.

A business will succeed only to the extent that the efforts of all are co-ordinated towards one result. At least one person is needed to direct all toward the desired end. The person at the head does not have to exactly outline to the others what steps to take, but he must possess the mental power of control over others.

An up-to-date business letter is not written in a casual, commonplace way today. The writer tries to convey something he thinks the receiver will be interested to know. In this way he awakens a responsive spirit. Sometimes just the addition of a word or two will change a letter of the matter-of-fact style to one that compels a response. It is not always what is actually in a letter, but the spirit which it breathes that brings results. That intangible something that defies analysis is the projected thought of the master that brings back the harvest that it claims.

But we should not always claim success for ourselves only. If you are anxious that some friend or relative should succeed, think of this person as becoming successful. Picture him in the position you would like to see him in. If he has a weakness, desire and command that it be strengthened; think of his shortcomings which belong to his negative nature as being replaced by positive qualities. Take a certain part of the day to send him thoughts of an up-building nature. You can in this way arouse his mental powers into activity, and once aroused, they will assert themselves and claim their own.

We can accomplish a great deal more than many of us are ready to believe by sending to another our direct, positive and controlling suggestions of leadership, but whether a man is a success or not is greatly determined by the way he acts on the suggestions he receives.

We either advance or decline. We never stand still. Every time we accomplish something it gives us ability to do greater things. The bigger the attempt undertaken, the greater the things accomplished in the future. As a business grows, the head of the business also has to grow. He must advance and be ever the guiding influence. By his power to control, he inspires confidence in those associated with him. Often employes are superior to their employers in some qualities, and, if they had studied, instead of neglected their development, they could have been employers of more commanding influence than those whom they serve.

Through your mental power you can generate in another enthusiasm and the spirit of success, which somehow furnishes an impetus to do something worth while.

In concentrated mental control, there is a latent power more potent than physical force. The person becomes aware that the attitude of the mind has a power of controlling, directing and governing other forces. He has been placed in an attitude capable of acquiring that which he desires.

All of us no matter how strong we are, are affected by the mental forces of our environment. There is no one that can remain neutral to influences. The mind cannot be freed from the forces of a place. If the environment of your place of business is not helpful, it will be harmful. That is why a change of position will often do a person a great deal of good.

No person was ever intended to live alone. If you are shut up with only your own thoughts you suffer from mental starvation. The mind becomes narrow; the mental powers weaken. Living alone often causes some of the milder forms of insanity. If children do not play with those their own age, but associate with only older people, they will take on the actions of the older people. The same is true of older persons if they associate with people younger than they are. They take on the spirit of youth. If you wish to retain your youth you need the influences of youth. Like attracts like all over the world.

The thought element plays a great part in our lives. Every business must not only command physical effort but it must also command thought effort. There must be co-ordination of thought. All employers should aim to secure employes that think along similar lines. They will work in fuller sympathy with each other. They will better understand each other. This enables them to help each other, which would be utterly impossible if they were not in sympathy with each other. It is this that goes to make up a perfect organization, which directs and influences them toward the one end. Instead of each person being a separate unit, each one is like a spoke in a big wheel. Each member carries his own load, and he would not think of shirking. Anyone working in such an atmosphere could not help turning out his best work.

All great leaders must be able to inspire this co-operative spirit. They first secure assistance through their mental control. They then make their assistants realize the value of mental control. Soon there is a close bond between them; they are working toward a single purpose. They profit by their combined effort. The result is that they accomplish much.

If your business is conducted in the right spirit, you can instill your thoughts and your ideas into your employes. Your methods and ideas become theirs. They don't know it, but your mental forces are shaping their work. They are just as certain to produce results as any physical force in nature.

The up-to-date business man of the future is going to take pains to get his employes to think and reason better. He will not want them to become depressed or discouraged. There is time that instead of being wasted he will endeavor to have them use in concentrated effort that will be profitable to both employer and employed. There must be more of the spirit of justice enter into the business of the future.

There is a firm I know that will not hire an employe until he has filled out an application blank. No doubt those that fill it out think it is foolishness, but it is not. A capable manager can look over this application blank and pretty nearly tell if this person will fit into his management. The main thing he wants to know is the applicant's capacity for efficient co-operative effort. He wants persons that have faith in themselves. He wants them to realize that when they talk of misfortunes and become blue they are likely to communicate the same depressing influence to others. The up-to-date manager wants to guard against hiring employes who will obstruct his success.

You must realize that every moment spent in thinking of your difficulties of the past, every moment spent in bad company is attracting to you all that is bad; is attracting influences that must be shaken off before you can advance.

Many firms prefer to hire employes that never worked before so that they have nothing to unlearn. They are then not trained, but have no bad business habits to overcome. They are more easily guided and grasp the new methods more effectively because they are not contrary to what they have already learned. They are at once started on the right road, and as they co-operate readily they receive the mental support of the management in learning the methods that have been perfected. This inspires confidence in themselves and they soon become efficient and, finally, skilled workers.

Most big business firms today employ efficiency experts. Each day or week they are in a different department. They earn their money because they familiarize persons with very little business experience with plans that has taken the "expert" years of training and much money to perfect.

The attitude we take has a great deal more to do with our success than most of us realize. We must be able to generate those forces that are helpful. There is a wonderful power in the thought rightly controlled and projected and we must through concentration develop this power to the fullest possible extent.

We are surrounded by many forces of which we know but little at present. Our knowledge of these is to be wonderfully increased. Each year we learn more about these psychic forces which are full of possibilities of which we are not even dimly conscious. We must believe in mental control, learn more about it, and use it, if we want to command these higher powers and forces which will unquestionably direct the lives of countless future generations.

LESSON XIX

A Concentrated will Development

New Method. You will find in this chapter a most effective and most practical method of developing the will. You can develop a strong one if you want to. You can make your Will a dynamo to draw to you untold power. Exercises are given which will, if practiced, strengthen your will, just as you would strengthen your muscles by athletic exercises.

In starting to do anything, we must first commence with elementary principles. Simple exercises will be given. It is impossible to estimate the ultimate good to be derived from the mental cultivation that comes through these attempts at concentration. Even the simple exercises are not to be thought useless. "In no respect," writes Doctor Oppenheim, "can a man show a finer quality of will-power than in his own private, intimate life." We are all subjected to certain temptations. The Will decides whether we will be just, or unjust; pure of thought; charitable in opinion; forbearing in overlooking other's shortcomings; whether we live up to our highest standard. Since these are all controlled by the Will, we should find time for plenty of exercises for training of the will in our daily life.

You, of course, realize that your will should be trained. You must also realize that to do this requires effort that you alone can command. No one can call it forth for you.

To be successful in these exercises you must practice them in a spirit of seriousness and earnestness. I can show you how to train your will, but your success depends upon your mastery and application of these methods.

New Methods of Will-Training. Select a quiet room where you will not be interrupted; have a watch to determine the time, and a note-book in which to enter observations. Start each exercise with date and time of day.

Exercise 1

Time decided on. Select some time of the day when most convenient. Sit in a chair and look at the door-knob for ten minutes. Then write down what you experienced. At first it will seem strange and unnatural. You will find it hard to hold one position for ten minutes. But keep as still as you can. The time will seem long for it will probably be the first time you ever sat and did nothing for ten minutes. You will find your thoughts wandering from the door-knob, and you will wonder what there can be in this exercise. Repeat this exercise for six days.

10 P. M. 2nd Day.

Notes. You should be able to sit quieter, and the time should pass more quickly. You will probably feel a little stronger because of gaining a better control of your will. It will brace you up, as you have kept your resolution. 10 P. M. 3rd Day.

Notes. It may be a little harder for you to concentrate on the door-knob as perhaps you had a very busy day and your mind kept trying to revert to what you had been doing during the day. Keep on trying and you will finally succeed in banishing all foreign thoughts. Then you should feel a desire to gain still more control. There is a feeling of power that comes over you when you are able to carry out your will. This exercise will make you feel bigger and it awakens a sense of nobility and manliness. You will say, "I find that I can actually do what I want to and can drive foreign thoughts out. The exercise, I can now see, is valuable."

10 P. M. 4th Day.

Notes. "I found that I could look at the door-knob and concentrate my attention on it at once. Have overcome the tendency to move my legs. No other thoughts try to enter as I have established the fact that I can do what I want to do and do not have to be directed. I feel that I am gaining in mental strength, I can now see the wonderful value of being the master of my own will-force. I know now if I make a resolution I will keep it. I have more self-confidence and can feel my self-control increasing.

10 P. M. 5th Day.

Notes. "Each day I seem to increase the intensity of my concentration. I feel that I can center my attention on anything I wish.10 P. M. 6th Day.

Notes. "I can instantly center my whole attention on the door-knob. Feel that I have thoroughly mastered this exercise and that I am ready for another."

You have practiced this exercise enough, but before you start another I want you to write a summary of just how successful you were in controlling the flitting impulses of the mind and will. You will find this an excellent practice. There is nothing more beneficial to the mind than to pay close attention to its own wonderful, subtle activities.

Exercise 2

Secure a package of playing cards. Select some time to do the exercise. Each day at the appointed time, take the pack in one hand and then start laying them down on top of each other just as slowly as you can, with an even motion. Try to get them as even as possible. Each card laid down should completely cover the under one. Do this exercise for six days.

1st Day.

Notes. Task will seem tedious and tiresome. Requires the closest concentration to make each card completely cover the preceding one. You will probably want to lay them down faster. It requires patience to lay them down so slowly, but benefit is lost if not so placed. You will find that at first your motions will be jerky and impetuous. It will require a little practice before you gain an easy control over your hands and arms. You probably have never tried to do anything in such a calm way. It will require the closest attention of your will. But you will find that you are acquiring a calmness you never had before. You are gradually acquiring new powers. You recognize how impulsive and impetuous you have been, and how, by using your will, you can control your temperament.

2nd Day.

Notes. You start laying the cards down slowly. You will find that by practice you can lay them down much faster. But you want to lay them down slowly and therefore you have to watch yourself. The slow, steady movement is wearisome. You have to conquer the desire of wanting to hurry up. Soon you will find that you can go slowly or fast at will.

3rd Day.

Notes. You still find it hard to go slowly. Your will urges you to go faster. This is especially true if you are impulsive, as the impulsive character finds it very difficult to do anything slowly and deliberately. It goes against the "grain." This exercise still is tiresome. But when you do it, it braces you up mentally. You are accomplishing something you do not like to do. It teaches you how to concentrate on disagreeable tasks. Writing these notes down you will find very helpful.

4th Day.

Notes. I find that I am beginning to place the cards in a mathematical way. I find one card is not completely covering another. I am getting a little careless and must be more careful. I command my will to concentrate more. It does not seem so hard to bring it under control.

5th Day.

Notes. I find that I am overcoming my jerky movements, that I can lay the cards down slowly and steadily. I feel that I am rapidly gaining more poise. I am getting better control over my will each day, and my will completely controls my movements. I begin to look on my will as a great governing power. I would not think of parting with the knowledge of will I have gained. I find it is a good exercise and know it will help me to accomplish my tasks.

6th Day.

Notes. I begin to feel the wonderful possibilities of the will. It gives me strength to think of the power of will. I am able to do so much more and better work now, that I realize that I can control my will action. Whatever my task, my will is concentrated on it. I am to keep my will centered there until the task is finished. The more closely and definitely I determine what I shall do, the more easily the will carries it out. Determination imparts compelling force to the will. It exerts itself more. The will and the end act and react on each other.

7th Day.

Notes. Now try to do everything you do today faster. Don't hurry or become nervous. Just try to do everything faster, but in a steady manner.

You will find that the exercises you have practiced in retardation have steadied your nerves, and thereby made it possible to increase your speed. The will is under your command. Make it carry out resolutions rapidly. This is how you build up your self-control and your self-command. It is then that the human machine acts as its author dictates.

You certainly should now be able to judge of the great benefit that comes from writing out your introspections each day. Of course you will not have the exact experiences given in these examples, but some of these will fit your case. Be careful to study your experiences carefully and make as true a report as you can. Describe your feelings just as they seem to you. Allow your fancies to color your report and it will be worthless. You have pictured conditions as you see them. In a few months, if you again try the same exercises, you will find your report very much better. By these introspections, we learn to know ourselves better and with this knowledge can wonderfully increase our efficiency. As you become used to writing out your report, it will be more accurate. You thus learn how to govern your impulses, activities and weaknesses.

Each person should try to plan exercises that will best fit his needs. If not convenient for you to practice exercises every day, take them twice or three times a week. But carry out any plan you decide to try. If you cannot devote ten minutes a day to the experiments start with five minutes and gradually increase the time. The exercises given are only intended for examples.

Will Training Without Exercise. There are many people that do not want to take the time to practice exercises, so the following instructions for training the will are given to them.

By willing and realizing, the will grows. Therefore the more you will, the more it grows, and builds up power. No matter whether your task is big or small, make it a rule to accomplish it in order to fortify your will. Form the habit of focusing your will in all its strength upon the subject to be achieved. You form in this way the habit of getting a thing done, of carrying out some plan. You acquire the feeling of being able to accomplish that which lies before you, no matter what it is. This gives you confidence and a sense of power that you get in no other way. You know when you make a resolution that you will keep it. You do not tackle new tasks in a half-hearted way, but with a bold, brave spirit. We know that the will is able to carry us over big obstacles. Knowing this despair never claims us for a victim. We have wills and are going to use them with more and more intensity, thus giving us the power to make our resolutions stronger, our actions freer and our lives finer and better.

The education of the will should not be left to chance. It is only definite tasks that will render it energetic, ready, persevering and consistent. The only way it can be done is by self-study and self-discipline. The cost is effort, time and patience, but the returns are valuable. There are no magical processes leading to will development, but the development of your will works wonders for you because it gives you self-mastery, personal power and energy of character.

Concentration of the Will to Win. The adaptability of persons to their business environment is more a matter of determination than anything else. In this age we hear a good deal of talk about a man's aptitudes. Some of his aptitudes, some of his powers, may be developed to a wonderful extent, but he is really an unknown quality until all his latent powers are developed to their highest possible extent. He may be a failure in one line and a big success in another. There are many successful men, that did not succeed well at what they first undertook, but they profited by their efforts in different directions, and this fitted them for higher things, whereas had they refused to adjust themselves to their environment, the tide of progress would have swept them into oblivion.

My one aim in all my works is to try and arouse in the individual the effort and determination to develop his full capacities, his highest possibilities. One thing I want you to realize at the start, that it is not so much ability, as it is the will to do that counts. Ability is very plentiful, but organizing initiative and creative power are not plentiful. It is easy to get employes, but to get someone to train them is harder. Their abilities must be directed to the work they can do. They must be shown how, while at this work, to conserve their energy and they must be taught to work in harmony with others, for most business concerns are dominated by a single personality.

Concentrating on Driving Force Within. We are all conscious, at times, that we have somewhere within us an active driving force that is ever trying to push us onward to better deeds. It is that "force" that makes us feel determined at times to do something worth while. It is not thought, emotion or feeling. This driving force is something distinct from thought or emotion. It is a quality of the soul and therefore it has a consciousness all its own. It is the "I will do" of the will. It is the force that makes the will concentrate. Many have felt this force working within them, driving them on to accomplish their tasks. All great men and women become conscious that this supreme and powerful force is their ally in carrying out great resolutions.

This driving force is within all, but until you reach a certain stage you do not become aware of it. It is most useful to the worthy. It springs up naturally without any thought of training. It comes unprovoked and leaves unnoticed. Just what this force is we do not know, but we do know that it is what intensifies the will in demanding just and harmonious action.

The ordinary human being, merely as merchandise, if he could be sold as a slave, would be worth ten thousand dollars. If somebody gave you a five thousand dollar automobile you would take very good care of it. You wouldn't put sand in the carburetor, or mix water with the gasoline, or drive it furiously over rough roads, or leave it out to freeze at night.

Are you quite sure that you take care of your own body, your own health, your only real property, as well as you would take care of a five thousand dollar automobile if it were given to you?

The man who mixes whiskey with his blood is more foolish than a man would be if he mixed water with gasoline in his car.

You can get another car; you cannot get another body.

The man who misses sleep lives irregularly—bolts his food so that his blood supply is imperfect. That is a foolish man treating himself as he would not treat any other valuable piece of property.

Do you try to talk with men and women who know more than you do, and do you LISTEN rather than try to tell them what you know?

There are a hundred thousand men of fifty, and men of sixty, running along in the old rut, any one of whom could get out of it and be counted among the successful men if only the spark could be found to explode the energy within them now going to waste.

Each man must study and solve his own problem.

LESSON XX

Concentration Reviewed

In bringing this book to a close, I again want to impress you with the inestimable value of concentration, because those that lack this great power or, rather that fail to develop it, will generally suffer from poverty and unhappiness and their life's work will most often be a failure, while those that develop and use it will make the most of life's opportunities,

I have tried to make these lessons practical and I am sure that many will find them so. Of course the mere reading of them will not do you a great deal of good, but, if the exercises are practiced and worked out and applied to your own individual case, you should be able to acquire the habit of concentration in such measure as to greatly improve your work and increase your happiness.

But remember the best instruction can only help you to the extent to which you put it into practice. I have found it an excellent idea to read a book through first, and then re-read it, and when you come to an idea that appeals to you, stop and think about it, then if applicable to you, repeat it over and over, that you will be impressed by it. In this way you can form the habit of picking out all the good things you read and these will have a wonderful influence on your character.

In this closing chapter, I want to impress you to concentrate on what you do, instead of performing most of your work unconsciously or automatically, until you have formed habits that give you the mastery of your work and your life powers and forces.

Very often the hardest part of work is thinking about it. When you get right into it, it does not seem so disagreeable. This is the experience of many when they first commence to learn how to concentrate. So never think it a difficult task, but undertake it with the "I Will Spirit" and you will find that its acquirement will be as easy as its application will be useful.

Read the life of any great man, and you will generally find that the dominant quality that made him successful was the ability to concentrate. Study those that have been failures and you will often find that lack of concentration was the cause.

> "One thing at a time, and that done will
> Is a good rule as I can tell."

All men are not born with equal powers, but it is the way they are used that counts. "Opportunity knocks at every man's door." Those that are successful hear the knock and grasp the chance. The failures believe that luck and circumstances are against them. They always blame someone else instead of themselves for their lack of success. We get what is coming to us, nothing more or less. Anything within the universe is within your grasp. Just use your latent powers and it is yours. You are aided by both visible and invisible forces when you concentrate on either "to do" or "to be."

Everyone is capable of some concentration, for without it you would be unable to say or do anything. People differ in the power to concentrate because some are unable to Will to hold the thought in mind for the required time. The amount of determination used determines who has the strongest will. No one's is stronger than yours. Think of this whenever you go against a strong opponent.

Never say "I can't concentrate today." You can do it just the minute you say "I will." You can keep your thoughts from straying, just the same as you can control your arms. When once you realize this fact, you can train the will to concentrate on anything you wish. If it wanders, it is your fault. You are not utilizing your will. But, don't blame it on your will and say it is weak. The will is just the same whether you act as if it were weak or as if it were strong. When you act as if your will is strong you say, "I can." When you act as if it were weak you say, "I can't." It requires the same amount of effort, in each case.

Some men get in the habit of thinking "I can't" and they fail. Others think "I can" and succeed. So remember, it is for you to decide whether you will join the army of "I can't" or "I can."

The big mistake with so many is that they don't realize that when they say "I can't," they really say, "I won't try." You can not tell what you can do until you try. "Can't" means you will not try.

Never say you cannot concentrate, for, when you do, you are really saying that you refuse to try.

Whenever you feel like saying, "I can't," say instead, "I possess all will and I can use as much as I wish." You only use as much as you have trained yourself to use.

An Experiment to Try. Before going to bed tonight, repeat, "I am going to choose my own thoughts, and to hold them as long as I choose. I am going to shut out all thoughts that weaken or interfere; that make me timid. My Will is as strong as anyone's else. While going to work the next morning, repeat this over. Keep this up for a month and you will find you will have a better opinion of yourself. These are the factors that make you a success. Hold fast to them always.

Concentration is nothing but willing to do a certain thing. All foreign thoughts can be kept out by willing that they stay out. You cannot realize your possibilities until you commence to direct your mind. You then do consciously what you have before done unconsciously. In this way you note mistakes, overcome bad habits and perfect your conduct.

You have at times been in a position that required courage and you were surprised at the amount you showed. Now, when once you arouse yourself, you have this courage all the time and it is not necessary to have a special occasion reveal it to you. My object in so strongly impressing this on your mind is to make you aware that the same courage, the same determination that you show at certain exceptionable times you have at your command at all times. It is a part of your vast resources. Use it often and well, in working out the highest destiny of which you are capable.

Final Concentration Instruction. You now realize that, in order to make your life worthy, useful and happy, you must concentrate. A number of exercises and all the needed instruction has been given. It now remains for you to form the highest ideal that you can in the present and live up to that ideal, and try to raise it. Don't waste your time in foolish reading. Select something that is inspiring, that you may become enrapport with those that think thoughts that are worth while. Their enthusiasm will inspire and enlighten you. Read slowly and concentrate on what you are reading. Let your spirit and the spirit of the author commune, and you will then sense what is between the lines—those great things which words cannot express.

Pay constant attention to one and one thing only for a given time and you will soon be able to concentrate. Hang on to that thought ceaselessly until you have attained your object. When you work, let your mind dwell steadily on your task. Think before you speak and direct your conversation to the subject under discussion. Do not ramble. Talk slowly, steadily and connectedly. Never form the hurry habit, but be deliberate in all you do. Assume static attitudes without moving a finger or an eyelid, or any part of your body. Read books that treat of but one continuous subject. Read long articles and recall the thread of the argument. Associate yourself with people who are steady, patient and tireless in their thought, action and work. See how long you can sit still and think on one subject without interruption.

Concentrating on the Higher Self. Father Time keeps going on and on. Every day he rolls around means one less day for you on this planet. Most of us only try to master the external conditions of this world. We think our success and happiness depends on us doing so. These are of course important and I don't want you to think they are not, but I want you to realize that when death comes, only those inherent and acquired qualities and conditions within the mentality—your character, conduct and soul growth—will go with you. If these are what they should be, you need not be afraid of not being successful and happy, for with these qualities you can mold external materials and conditions.

Study yourself. Find Your Strong Points And Make Them Stronger As Well As Yo Weak Ones And Strengthen Them. Study yourself carefully and you will see yourself as you really are.

The secret of accomplishment is concentration, or the art of turning all your power upon just one point at a time.

If you have studied yourself carefully you should have a good line on yourself, and should be able to make the proper interior re-adjustments. Remember first, last, and always, Right thinking and right Living necessarily results in happiness, and it is therefore within your power to obtain happiness. Anyone that is not happy does not claim their birthright.

Keep in mind that some day you are going to leave this world and think of what you will take with you. This will assist you to concentrate on the higher forces. Now start from this minute, to act according to the advice of the higher self in everything you do. If you do, its ever harmonious forces will necessarily insure to you a successful fulfilment of all your life purposes. Whenever you feel tempted to disobey your higher promptings, hold the thought

"My-higher-self-insures-to-me-the-happiness-of-doing-that-which -best-answers-my-true-relations-to-all-others."

You possess latent talents, that when developed and utilized are of assistance to you and others. But if you do not properly use them, you shirk your duty, and you will be the loser and suffer from the consequences. Others will also be worse off if you do not fulfil your obligations.

When you have aroused into activity your thought powers you will realize the wonderful value of these principles in helping you to carry out your plans. The right in the end must prevail. You can assist in the working out of the great plan of the universe and thereby gain the reward, or you can work against the great plan and suffer the consequences. The all consuming fires are gradually purifying all discordant elements. If you choose to work contrary to the law you will burn in its crucible, so I want you to learn to concentrate intelligently on becoming in harmony with your higher self. Hold the thought: "I-will-live-for-my-best. I-seek-wisdom, self-knowledge, happiness-and-power-to-help-others. I-act-from-the-higher-self, therefore-only-the-best-can-come-to-me. The more we become conscious of the presence of the higher self the more we should try to become a true representative of the human soul in all its wholeness and holiness, instead of wasting our time dwelling on some trifling external quality or defect. We should try to secure a true conception of what we really are so as not to over value the external furnishings. You will then not surrender your dignity or self respect, when others ignorantly make a display of material things to show off. Only the person that realizes that he is a permanent Being knows what the true self is.

THE END.

Printed in the United States
149940LV00002B/7/A

9 788184 561616